Integrating the Curricula: A Collection

Edited By
Robin Fogarty

IRI/Skylight Publishing, Inc.
Palatine, Illinois

Integrating the Curricula: A Collection
First Printing

Published by IRI/Skylight Publishing, Inc.
200 E. Wood Street, Suite 274
Palatine, Illinois 60067
Phone 800-348-4474, 708-991-6300
FAX 708-991-6420

Creative Director: Robin Fogarty
Editors: Liesl Banks-Stiegman, Erica Pochis, Julia E. Noblitt
Type Compositor: Donna Ramirez
Book Designers: Michael Melasi, Bruce Leckie
Production Coordinators: David Stockman, Amy Behrens

Library of Congress Catalog Card Number: 93-80674
Printed in the United States of America
ISBN 0-932935-37-0

0676-12-93

Table of Contents

Introduction

Integrating the Curricula: A Collection

Do not confine your children to your own learning
For they were born in another time!—Hebrew Proverb

The call for curriculum integration is both timely and wide-spread. The time is right and the need is pressing, for we are living in an age when information doubles every year and a half; when futurists predict that today's seven-year-old will experience at least seven major career shifts in a lifetime; when neurologists reveal how the brain literally grows dendrites when stimulated; when cognitive psychologists discard the theory of fixed IQ and present a spectrum of multiple intelligences; when technology is changing the fields of study so rapidly that a university professor laments to his pre-med students, "By the time you graduate and become practicing physicians, fifty percent of what we've taught you will be obsolete...and we don't know which fifty percent."

In response to these societal trends, educators, community and business leaders, and learners themselves are searching for ways to create forms of schooling that are more holistic and natural; more integrated and interwoven. With that in mind, the purpose of this collection is to pull together, under one cover, the multifaceted concept of curriculum integration.

Just as with any emerging idea, questions abound and the answers seem somewhat elusive. In this book, leading voices in the field, those of the researchers and theorists, as well as those of the front-line practitioners, combine to shed light on this complex topic.

Sections 1 and 2, "Curriculum Integration: An Invitation to Learn" and "Curriculum Overview: What's the Big Picture?" explore reasons and rationale for moving toward more holistic models of learning. Section 3 places the concept of curriculum integration squarely in the present, but frames it in a significant historical perspective by proclaiming "It's not new!"

Section 4 presents practical models for planning integrated curriculum while Section 5 showcases actual school programs in a section entitled, "Integrated Learning: Ideas in Practice."

Finally, the subtleties of the integration process itself are illuminated in Section 6, "Teacher Teams: Beginning the Conversations." The book closes with a critical look at the concept from the eyes of a critic and from the eyes of the students themselves. These diverging portrayals comprise Section 7, "The Final Analysis: Two Views."

Each section is prefaced with a brief introduction to the essays included. Readers are invited to proceed sequentially through the book from the beginning to the end or to dip in and out of the book, sampling sections that target personally relevant concerns. This collection brings into focus the multiple dimensions of integrating curricula as the educational community finds practical ways to create schooling that makes sense.

Curriculum Integration: An Invitation to Learn

Education and the process of educating is a total integral, contextual situation which includes students, teachers, parents, administration and environment. —Jean Houston, *Millennium: Glimpses into the 21st Century*, 1981, p. 159.

The invitation to change is received differently by the various members of the educational community. Some never receive the invitation; others claim they weren't invited; still more are invited, but choose not to attend; a few are invited and are going; and then there are those who are actually giving the party. Let's look more closely at these groups.

There are those who never get the invitation; often they don't even know that an event of consequence is in progress. These people are totally unaware, oblivious to current research and its implications for schools. They are silent and seem somewhat insulated from the changing world.

Then, there are those educators who claim they weren't invited. These are the people who charge that everything is done to them; that school reform is a top-down mandate; that they don't have a voice in the process. As a result , they *have no voice* in the process.

Another category of people are those who know they're invited, but proclaim loudly, "I'm not going! The educational pendulum swings to and fro. If I stay right here, it'll swing back to this point, again." These are the people who aggressively resist change.

Still another group are those who are looking for the invitation and accept it eagerly. These are the ones who grasp every opportunity to improve their professions and desire to renew their teaching spirit and instructional skills.

Finally, there are those who plan the party and write the invitations. These are the pro-active shakers and movers who press forward with ideas of substance and change. People who think, invent, and problem solve in a genuine effort to affect positive and lasting change in the field.

The invitation to change is examined in Section 1 with three essays that present convincing rationale for change. The first piece, from the perspective of the world of work, suggests that vocational education, an application-rich content, become an educational delivery system rather than merely a content area. Kolde explains that applied learning and hands-on experimentation encourages a posture of learning how to learn and that a linking of the academics to vocational studies into an integrated model makes sense.

Providing convincing evidence for curriculum integration is the second essay by Caine and Caine. The authors outline the current brain research that dictates a shift from traditionally fragmented models of curriculum to more natural and holistic systems. Their research on brain-based and brain-compatible learning supports integrated learning in current educational reform.

And, last in this somewhat lengthy article, Cummings addresses some major interdisciplinary issues such as recognizing the limits of models and thinking about what lies ahead. He cautions that, "We must never lose sight of the fact that disciplines are convenient but artificial constructs: academics may be divided into disciplines, but the world is not."

Integrated Learning for a Competitive Work Force

by Rosemary F. Kolde

Under the new definition, Ms. Kolde suggests, vocational education becomes an educational delivery system—not a content area. Using a variety of approaches, such as applied learning and experimentation, the system encourages students to learn how to learn.

To maintain a competitive edge in the global economy of the 1990s and beyond, the U.S. must capitalize on its human resources. The global economy is producing an extraordinary number of well-paying jobs, but these jobs have increasingly rigorous requirements for competencies and skills. Thus the challenge facing our nation is to educate and train our shrinking work force to prepare it for such jobs.

There is a growing gap between the skills demanded by the new economy and the skills available to meet those demands. New technology requires higher capabilities in reading and mathematics. Flexibility and adaptability are now prized qualities in workers, whereas in the past many jobs were routine and specialized. The shift from assembly-line production to cooperative work teams requires good communication skills. As Thomas Bailey noted in a report prepared for the National Center on Education and Employment and the National Center for Research in Vocational Education, "A new generation of research suggests that jobs of the future will require more skill and education, not less." He further states that there is "a shift toward finding better-educated middle-level workers who have a stronger capacity to comprehend."[1]

> **A new generation of research suggests that jobs of the future will require more skill and education, not less.**

From *Phi Delta Kappan*, vol. 72, no. 6, p. 453-455, February 1991. Reprinted with permission.

Changes in federal policy on vocational education also reflect the growing national concern about developing a qualified and competitive work force. Congress has attempted to deal with these issues through amendments to the Carl D. Perkins Vocational and Applied Technology Education Act. Following the trend in the more advanced vocational education institutions, Congress has called for the integration of academic and vocational education. The benefits to be derived from this integrated instruction include both a better-prepared work force and an improved education system.

If we are to maximize the potential of our nation's human resources, we must attract students of all ability levels to vocational education. To accomplish this objective, we must redefine vocational education, giving it a much broader focus and purpose. Under this new definition, vocational education becomes an educational delivery system—not a content area. Vocational education blends and interrelates all the various subject areas into an integrated and comprehensive educational program that emphasizes higher-order thinking and problem-solving skills. Using a variety of approaches, such as applied learning and experimentation, the system encourages students to learn how to learn.

A report by the Committee for Economic Development states: "Mastery of the old basics of reading, writing, and arithmetic may be sufficient for entry-level jobs, but because of the constantly changing nature of work, minimum skills are not sufficient preparation for career advancement. Schools must make a greater effort to develop higher-level skills such as problem-solving, reasoning, and learning ability."[2] The report further recommends that the mastery of basic skills and subject content should not be judged solely by a student's ability to pass an examination but should also be judged by how well the student can apply the skills.

Successful vocational education programs throughout the U.S. have strengthened their formats and have raised the required competencies in mathematics, science, communication, and organizational skills. These competencies are not isolated in theory-based academic programs but are correlated and integrated with technical occupational skills. Vocational education has traditionally provided an applied learning environment in which students participate in actual job tasks. Students learn to apply academic concepts in a real-world setting—the vocational laboratory with live work experience.

Students' success in acquiring basic skills may be dependent on their being able to use their preferred learning styles. Integrated academics can provide for learning through both an abstract approach and concrete application. Academic and vocational education are not in conflict but are complementary. Each serves distinct functions that often overlap.

THE INTEGRATED CURRICULUM

Sandra Pritz has defined the integration of academic and vocational instruction as "the linking of academic skills instruction to vocational applications to enhance student learning."[3] An opportunity for such integration would arise, for example, when culinary arts students study percentages in their mathematics class. The math teacher instructs the class on how to figure percentages and gives them a number of problems that involve the use of percentages in the food-service industry. The students are given diagrams showing how a side of beef is blocked out into different cuts, each weighing a certain number of pounds. They are then taught how to find the percentage of each wholesale or primal cut.

The culinary arts instructor then builds on the basic mathematical concept of percentages in the vocational laboratory by assigning the students the job of placing a restaurant order with the local slaughterhouse. Using information about the cuts needed and the weights of available sides of beef, they must determine whether it is more advantageous to purchase meat by the side or by the saddle.

The process of finding technical applications for academic skills must be a cooperative venture. Vocational and academic instructors work together to develop the curriculum, with input from business and industry. Involving both kinds of instructors in the planning sets the stage for change, develops the teachers' commitment to the resulting curriculum, and helps to build academic/vocational teams. In this cooperative process, vocational instructors complete job analyses and then identify the math and science concepts and skills that need to be taught for each block of instruction. Mathematics and science specialists use that information to develop an academic curriculum that dovetails with the vocational course of study.[4]

Academic and vocational instructors work together to design strategies, select materials and instructional methods, and develop activity guides, job-plan sheets, and other supportive instructional materials for students and teachers. This cooperation continues after the development phase, with weekly meetings of the instructors to discuss procedures, student achievement, new thoughts and concepts, and other relevant details. Team teaching is used when beneficial. Academic instructors regularly attend the vocational laboratories to observe how students apply the concepts that were introduced in the academic classes. The result is a learning process for both students and teachers.

Planning for an integrated curriculum is a change process that takes time. It is imperative to involve all the appropriate groups and individuals who will play key roles in this change.

The greater continuity in the curriculum enables students to progress at a more rapid pace. Moreover, the curriculum requires students to take more responsibility for their own learning, through individual work outside the class and through such assignments as the preparation of job-plan sheets, which give directions for carrying out the operations or procedures involved in completing a job.

Planning for an integrated curriculum is a change process that takes time. It is imperative to involve all the appropriate groups and individuals who will play key roles in this change. Their needs and concerns must be addressed at each stage of the process, because everyone must buy into an integrated curriculum if the concept is to be successful.

What are the specific benefits of an integrated curriculum?

• When academic and vocational instructors cooperate in the development of instructional materials, such as learning guides and job-plan sheets, the materials are better organized and of higher quality.

• The cooperative effort of the academic and vocational instructors to integrate mathematics and science concepts into the technical applications makes the curriculum more rigorous and gives it greater continuity.

• The application of both abstract and concrete approaches to learning enhances student knowledge.

• The more intensified curriculum and the use of learning activity guides enable students to progress at their own pace.

• The cooperatively developed materials help the students to be better prepared in class to complete tasks and solve problems.

• When the instructional staff works together, the students benefit from having access to several experts rather than just one.

• Students score higher on paper-and-pencil achievement tests and on tests of technical performance.

• Students are more highly motivated and have lower rates of absenteeism.

At a conference titled "The Quality Connection: Linking Education and Work," jointly sponsored by the Department of Labor and the Department of Education in May 1990, each of the keynote speakers emphasized that the integration of academics and vocational education is imperative. Lauro Cavazos, then U.S. secretary of education, indicated that the best approach toward the goal of achieving universal competency in basic skills may be to "integrate academic and vocational teaching methods into new applied curricula for *all* students."[5]

Business and industry have long recognized the need for employees who possess a solid foundation in the academic basics, who can communicate with and relate to one another, and who are competent in the basic technical skills of the occupation. As the economy has changed its focus from production to service to information, the composition of the work force has become increasingly diverse, and the scope of required skills has expanded. To meet the needs of the workplace, education must change. The classroom of the future is one that integrates academic and technical knowledge and skills within an applied vocational learning model. This model makes good educational and economic sense and will prove, as the history of education reform is written, to have been a most valuable design.

NOTES

1. Thomas Bailey, "Jobs of the Future and Skills They Will Require," *American Educator*, Spring 1990, p. 10-15.
2. *Investing in Our Children* (Washington, DC: Committee for Economic Development, 1985), p. 16.
3. Sandra G. Pritz, "Basics for Students At-Risk—A Vocational-Academic Approach," paper presented at the North Central Regional Educational Laboratory Conference on At-Risk Students, Chicago, 1988.

4. Lois G. Harrington, "Making Common Sense: Integrating Academic and Vocational Studies," in *Curriculum Report*, National Association of Secondary School Principals, Reston, VA, September 1988.
5. "School-to-Work Conference Focuses on Vocational Education Reform," *Update*, American Vocational Association, Alexandria, VA, June 1990.

Understanding a Brain-Based Approach to Learning and Teaching

by Renate Nummela Caine and Geoffrey Caine

Educators who become aware of recent research on how the brain learns will gain exciting ideas about conditions and environments that can optimize learning.

The greatest challenge of brain research for educators does not lie in understanding the anatomical intricacies of brain functioning but in comprehending the vastness, complexity, and potential of the human brain. What we are beginning to discover about the role of emotions, stress, and threat in learning and about memory systems and motivation is challenging basic assumptions about traditional education. Fully understood, this information requires a major shift in our definitions of testing and grading and in the organizational structure of classrooms and schools.

> What we are beginning to discover about the role of emotions, stress, and threat in learning and about memory systems and motivation is challenging basic assumptions about traditional education.

PRINCIPLES FOR BRAIN-BASED LEARNING

We offer the following brain principles as a general theoretical foundation for brain-based learning. These principles are simple and neurologically sound. Applied to education, however, they help us reconceptualize teaching by taking us out of traditional frames

From *Educational Leadership*, vol. 48, no. 2, p. 66-70, 1990.
Reprinted with permission.

of reference and guiding us in defining and selecting appropriate programs and methodologies.

Principle One: The Brain Is a Parallel Processor

The brain ceaselessly performs many functions simultaneously (Ornstein and Thompson 1984). Thoughts, emotions, imagination, and predispositions operate concurrently. They interact with other brain processes such as health maintenance and the expansion of general social and cultural knowledge.

Implications for education: Like the brain, good teaching should "orchestrate" all the dimensions of parallel processing, and it must be based on theories and methodologies that make such orchestration possible. As no one method or technique can by itself adequately encompass the variations of the human brain, teachers need a frame of reference that enables them to select from the vast array of methods and approaches that are available.

Principle Two: Learning Engages the Entire Physiology

Like the heart, liver, or lungs, the brain is an incredibly complex physiological organ functioning according to physiological rules. Learning is as natural as breathing, and it is possible to either inhibit or facilitate it. Neuron growth, nourishment, and synaptic interactions are integrally related to the perception and interpretation of experiences (Diamond 1985). Stress and threat affect the brain, and it is influenced differently by peace, challenge, boredom, happiness, and contentment (Ornstein and Sobel 1987). In fact, the actual "wiring" of the brain is affected by school and life experiences. Anything that affects our physiological functioning affects our capacity to learn.

Implications for education: Brain-based teaching must fully incorporate stress management, nutrition, exercise, drug education, and other facets of health into the learning process. Learning is influenced by the natural development of the body and the brain. According to brain research, for example, there can be a five-year difference in maturation between any two "average" children. Gauging achievement on the basis of chronological age is therefore inappropriate.

Principle Three: The Search for Meaning Is Innate

The search for meaning (making sense of our experiences) is survival oriented and basic to the human brain. The brain needs and automatically registers the familiar while simultaneously searching for and responding to novel stimuli (O'Keefe and Nadel 1978). This dual process is taking place every waking moment (and, some contend, while sleeping). Other brain research confirms the idea that people are "meaning makers" (see, e.g., Springer and Deutsch 1985, p. 33). The search for meaning cannot be stopped, only channeled and focused.

Implications for education: Brain-based education must furnish a learning environment that provides stability and familiarity. At the same time, it should be able to satisfy the brain's enormous curiosity and hunger for novelty, discovery, and challenge. Programs for gifted children already combine a rich environment with complex and meaningful challenges. Most of the creative methods used for teaching gifted students should be applied to all students.

Principle Four: The Search for Meaning Occurs Through "Patterning"

In a way, the brain is both scientist and artist, attempting to discern and understand patterns as they occur and giving expression to unique and creative patterns of its own (Lakoff 1987, Rosenfield 1988, Nummela and Rosengren 1986, Hart 1983). Designed to perceive and generate patterns, the brain resists having meaningless patterns imposed on it. By meaningless we mean isolated pieces of information that are unrelated to what makes sense to a particular student. When the brain's natural capacity to integrate information is acknowledged and invoked in teaching, vast amounts of initially related or seemingly random information and activities can be presented and assimilated.

Implications for education: Learners are patterning all the time in one way or another. We cannot stop them, we can only influence the direction. Daydreaming is a form of patterning, so are problem solving and critical thinking. Although we choose much of what students are to learn, we should, rather than attempt to impose patterns, present the information in a way that allows brains to extract patterns. "Time on task" does not ensure appropriate patterning because the student may actually be engaged in "busywork" while the mind is somewhere else. For teaching to be really effective, a learner must be able to create meaningful and personally relevant patterns. This type of teaching is most clearly recognized by those advocating a whole-language approach to reading (Goodman 1986; Altweger, Edelsky, and Flores 1987), thematic teaching, integration of the curriculum (Shalley 1988), and life-relevant approaches to learning.

Principle Five: Emotions Are Critical to Patterning

What we learn is influenced and organized by emotions and mind-sets involving expectancy, personal biases and prejudices, self-esteem, and the need for social interaction. Thus, emotions and cognition cannot be separated (Ornstein and Sobel 1987, Lakoff 1987, McGuinness and Pribram 1980, Halgren et al. 1983). Emotions are also crucial to memory because they facilitate the storage and recall of information (Rosenfield 1988). The emotional impact of any lesson or life experience may continue to reverberate long after the specific event that triggered it.

> The emotional impact of any lesson or life experience may continue to reverberate long after the specific event that triggered it.

Implications for education: Teachers must understand that students' feelings and attitudes will be involved in learning and will determine future learning. They should make sure that the emotional climate is supportive and marked by mutual respect and acceptance. Cooperative approaches to learning support this notion. Student and teacher reflection and metacognitive approaches should be encouraged. The emotional color of teacher-student encounters depends on the sincerity of the support that teachers, administrators, and students offer each other.

Principle Six: Every Brain Simultaneously Perceives and Creates Parts and Wholes

Although there *is* evidence of brain laterality, meaning that there are differences between the left and the right hemispheres of the brain (Springer and Deutsch 1985), left brain-right brain is not the whole story. In a healthy person the two hemispheres are inextricably interactive, irrespective of whether a person is dealing with words, mathematics, music, or art (Hand 1984, Hart 1975). The value of the "two-brain" doctrine is that it requires educators to acknowledge the brain's separate but simultaneous tendencies for organizing information. One is to reduce such information into parts; the other is to perceive and work with it as a whole or series of wholes.

Implications for Education: People have enormous difficulty learning when either parts or wholes are neglected. Good teaching builds understanding and skills over time because it recognizes that learning is cumulative and developmental. However, parts and wholes are conceptually interactive. They derive meaning from each other. Thus, vocabulary and grammar are best understood and mastered when they are incorporated in genuine, whole-language experiences. Similarly, equations and scientific principles are best dealt with in the context of living science.

Principle Seven: Learning Involves Both Focused Attention and Peripheral Perception

The brain absorbs the information of which it is directly aware and to which it is paying attention. It also directly absorbs information and signals that lie beyond the immediate focus of attention. These may be stimuli that one perceives "out of the side of the eyes" such as gray and unattractive walls in a classroom. Peripheral stimuli also include the very light or subtle signals that are within the field of attention but are still not consciously noticed (such as a hint of a smile or slight changes in body posture). This means that the brain responds to the entire sensory context in which teaching or communication occurs (O'Keefe and Nadel 1978). One of Lozanov's (1978a, 1978b) fundamental principles is that every stimulus is coded, associated, and symbolized by the brain. Every sound (from a word to a siren) and every visual signal (from a blank screen to a raised finger) is packed full of complex meanings. Peripheral information can therefore be purposely organized to facilitate learning.

Implications for education: The teacher can and should organize materials that will be outside the focus of the learner's attention. In addition to traditional concerns with noise, temperature, and so on, peripherals include visuals such as charts, illustrations, set designs, and art, including great works of art. Barzakov (1988) recommends that teachers change art frequently to reflect changes in learning focus. Music has also become very important as a means to enhance and influence more natural acquisition of information. The subtle signals that emanate from a teacher also have an impact on learning. Our inner states show in skin color, muscular tension and posture, rate of breathing, eye movements, and so on. Teachers should engage the interests and enthusiasm of students through their own enthusiasm, coaching, and modeling, so that the unconscious signals relating to the importance and value of what is being learned are appropriate. Lozanov (1978a, 1978b) coined the term "double planeness" to describe the congruence of the internal and external in a person—it is important to practice what we preach and to express genuine feelings rather than to fake them, because our true inner states are always signaled and discerned at some level by learners.

> We learn much more than we ever consciously understand. Most of the signals that we peripherally perceive enter the brain without our awareness and interact at unconscious levels.

Principle Eight: Learning Always Involves Conscious and Unconscious Processes

We learn much more than we ever consciously understand. Most of the signals that we peripherally perceive enter the brain without our awareness and interact at unconscious levels. "Having reached the brain, this information emerges in the consciousness with some delay, or it influences motives and decisions" (Lozanov 1978b). Thus, we remember what we experience, not just what we are told. A student can easily learn to sing on key and learn to hate singing at the same time. Teaching should therefore be designed in such a way as to help students benefit maximally from unconscious processing. In part this is done by addressing the peripheral context (as described above). In part it is done through instruction.

Implications for education: A great deal of the effort put into teaching and studying is wasted because students do not adequately process their experiences. "Active processing" allows students to review how and what they learned so that they can begin to take charge of their learning and the development of their own personal meanings. It refers to reflection and metacognitive activities—for example, a student might become aware of his or her preferred learning style. Teachers may facilitate active processing by creatively "elaborating" procedures and theories through metaphors and analogies to help students reorganize the material in personally meaningful and valuable ways.

Principle Nine: We Have Two Types of Memory: A Spatial Memory System and a Set of Systems for Rote Learning

We have a natural spatial memory system which does not need rehearsal and allows for "instant" memory of experiences (Nadel and Wilmer 1980, Nadel et al. 1984, Bransford and Johnson 1972). Remembering what we had for dinner last night does not require the use of memorization techniques. That is because we have at least one memory system actually designed for registering our experiences in ordinary three-dimensional space (O'Keefe and Nadel 1978). The system is always engaged and is inexhaustible. It is enriched over time as we increase our repertoire of natural categories and procedures (there was a time when we did not know what a tree or a televisions was). The system is motivated by novelty. In fact, this is one of the systems that drives the search for meaning.

Facts and skills that are dealt with in isolation are organized differently by the brain and need much more practice and rehearsal. The counterpart of the spatial memory system is a set of systems specifically designed for storing relative unrelated information (O'Keefe and Nadel 1978). The more information and skills are separated from prior knowledge and actual experience, the more we depend on rote memory and repetition. These systems operate according to the information processing model of memory which suggests that all new information must be worked on before it is stored. However, concentrating too heavily on the storage and recall of unconnected facts is a very inefficient use of the brain.

Implications for education: Educators are adept at focusing on memorization of facts. Common examples include multiplication tables, spelling, and sets of principles in different subjects. However, an overemphasis on such procedures leaves the learner impoverished, does not facilitate the transfer of learning, and probably interferes with the development of understanding. By ignoring the personal world of the learner, educators actually inhibit the effective functioning of the brain.

Principle Ten: The Brain Understands and Remembers Best When Facts and Skills Are Embedded in Natural Spatial Memory

Our native language is learned through multiple interactive experiences involving vocabulary and grammar. It is shaped both by internal processes and by social interaction (Vygotsky 1978). That is an example of how specific items are given meaning when embedded in ordinary experiences. Education is enhanced when this type of embedding is adopted. Embedding is the single most important element that the new brain-based theories of learning have in common.

> Success depends on making use of all the senses by immersing the learner in a multitude of complex and interactive experiences.

Implications for education: The embedding process is complex because it depends on all the other principles discussed above. Spatial memory is generally best invoked through experiential learning, an approach that is valued more highly in some cultures than in others. Teachers should use a great deal of "real life" activity including classroom demonstrations, projects, field trips, visual imagery of certain experiences and best performances, stories, metaphor, drama, interaction of different subjects, and so on. Vocabulary can be "experienced" through skits. Grammar can be learned "in process" through stories or writing. Mathematics, science, and history can be integrated so that much more information is understood and absorbed than is presently the norm. Success depends on making use of all the senses by immersing the learner in a multitude of complex and interactive experiences. Teachers should not exclude lectures and analysis, but they should make them part of a larger experience.

Principle Eleven: Learning Is Enhanced by Challenge and Inhibited by Threat

The brain learns optimally when appropriately challenged, but "down-shifts" under perceived threat (Hart 1983). In the language of phenomenology, we narrow the perceptual field when threatened (Combs and Snygg 1959) by becoming less flexible and by reverting to automatic and often more primitive routine behaviors. The hippocampus, a part of the limbic system, appears to function partially as a relay center to the rest of the brain. It is the part of the brain most sensitive to stress (Jacobs and Nadel 1985). Under perceived threat, we literally lose access to portions of our brain, probably because of the extreme sensitivity of the hippocampus.

> The objective of brain-based learning is to move from memorizing information to meaningful learning. This requires that three interactive elements be present: relaxed alertness, immersion, and active processing.

Implications for education: Teachers and administrators should strive to create a state of relaxed alertness in students. This means that they need to provide an atmosphere that is low in threat and high in challenge. This state must continuously pervade the lessons and must be present in the teacher. All the methodologies the teacher uses to orchestrate the learning context influence the state of relaxed alertness.

Principle Twelve: Each Brain Is Unique

Although we all have the same set of systems, including our senses and basic emotions, they are integrated differently in each and every brain. In addition, because learning actually changes the structure of the brain, the more we learn, the more unique we become.

Implications for education: Teaching should be multifaceted in order to allow all students to express visual, tactile, emotional, or auditory preferences. Choices should also be variable enough to attract individual interests. This may require the reshaping of learning organizations so that they exhibit the complexity found in life. In sum, education needs to facilitate optimal brain functioning.

What Schools Should Do

The objective of brain-based learning is to move from memorizing information to meaningful learning. This requires that three interactive elements be present: relaxed alertness, immersion, and active processing (Caine and Caine 1989).

Relaxed alertness as a state of mind meets the brain's preference for challenge and its search for meaning. Teachers should provide an atmosphere that combines a sense of low threat with significant challenge and the degree of relaxation characteristic of people who are confident and at ease with themselves. This is a delicate balance.

Teachers should orchestrate the immersion of their students in appropriate experiences because all learning is experiential in some sense and because it is the sense that students make of their experience as a whole that determines the degree of learning. Class and school curriculums should overlap. Educators can integrate subjects such as science, mathematics, history, and reading. They can make their schools into small, healthy, "real-world" communities where students, young and old alike, are given responsibilities for handling ceremonies, news flyers, clean-up, and supervisory functions (such as zookeeper, head gardener, and public relations person).

Active processing, through such activities as questioning and genuine reflection, allows learners to take charge of the consolidation and internalization of learning in a way that is personally meaningful. Students may keep a personal journal, for example, leaving the way open for their brains to see things in a new light. Active processing also allows students to recognize and deal with their own biases and attitudes and to develop thinking skills and logic as they search for broader implications and connections for what they are learning. These techniques for metacognition and reflection are very sophisticated and take a more concrete form in the lower grades.

Understanding how the brain learns has implications for instructional design, administration, evaluation, the role of the school in the community, teacher education, and a host of other issues critical to educational reform. The evidence suggests not only that we learn from experiences but that there is much more to this process than we have appreciated. Acknowledging how the brain learns from experiences will help us to understand meaningful learning more fully. In that sense, brain-based learning is not a separate thrust or movement in education; it is an approach from which all education will ultimately benefit.

REFERENCES

Altweger, B., C. Edelsky, and B. Flores. (1987). "Whole Language: What's New?" *The Reading Teacher 41*, 2: 144-154.

Barzakov, I. (July 14, 1988). *Optimalearning* (tm) Workshop. Unpublished workshop notes.

Bransford, D.J., and M.V. Johnson (1972). "Contextual Prerequisites for Understanding: Some Investigations of Comprehensive Recall." *Journal of Verbal Learning and Verbal Behavior 11*: 717-721.

Caine, G., and R.N. Caine. (May 1989). "Learning about Accelerated Learning." *Training and Development Journal*: 65-73.

Combs, A.W., and D. Snygg. (1959). *Individual Behavior: A Perceptual Approach to Behavior.* New York: Harper & Row.

Diamond, M.C. (March 23, 1985). *Brain Growth in Response to Experience.* Seminar, University of California, Riverside.

Goodman, K. (1986). *What's Whole in Whole Language?* Portsmouth, N.H.: Heinemann.

Halgren, E., C.L. Wilson, N.K. Squires, J. Engel, R.D. Walter, and P.II. Crandall. (1983). "Dynamics of the Hippocampal Contribution to Memory: Stimulation and Recording Studies in Humans." In *Molecular, Cellular, and Behavioral Neurobiology of the Hippocampus*, edited by W. Seifert. New York: Academic Press.

Hand, J.D. (1984). "Split Brain Theory and Recent Results in Brain Research: Implications for the Design of Instruction." In *Instructional Development: The State of the Art, II*, edited by R.K. Bass and C.R. Dills. Dubuque, Iowa: Kendall/Hunt.

Hart, L. (1975). *How the Brain Works.* New York: Basic Books.

Hart, L. (1983). *Human Brain, Human Learning.* New York: Longman, Inc.

Jacobs, W.J., and L. Nadel. (1985). "Stress-Induced Recovery of Fears and Phobias." *Psychological Review 92*, 4: 512-531.

Lakoff, G. (1987). *Women, Fire, and Dangerous Things.* Chicago: The University of Chicago Press.

Lozanov, G. (1978a). *Suggestology and Outlines of Suggestopedy.* New York: Gordon and Breach.

Lozanov, G. (1978b). *Suggestology and Suggestopedia—Theory and Practice.* Working document for the Expert Working Group, United Nations Educational Scientific and Cultural Organization (UNESCO). (ED-78/WS/ 119)

McGuinness, D. and K. Pribram. (1980). "The Neuropsychology of Attention, Emotional and Motivational Controls." In *The Brain and Psychology,* edited by M.C. Wittrock. New York Academic Press.

Nadel, L. and J. Wilmer. (1980). "Context and Conditioning: A Place for Space." *Physiological Psychology 8*: 218-228.

Nadel, L., J. Wilmer, and E.M. Kurz. (1984). "Cognitive Maps and Environmental Context." In *Context and Learning,* edited by P. Balsam and A. Tomi. Hillsdale, N.J.: Lawrence Erlbaum Assoc.

Nummela, R.M., and T.M. Rosengren. (1986). "What's Happening in Students Brains May Redefine Teaching." *Educational Leadership 43*: 49-53.

O'Keefe, J., and L. Nadel. (1978). *The Hippocampus as a Cognitive Map.* Oxford: Clarendon Press.

Ornstein, R., and R. Thompson. (1984). *The Amazing Brain.* Boston: Houghton Mifflin Company.

Ornstein, R., and D. Sobel. (1987). *The Healing Brain.* New York: Simon and Schuster, Inc.

Pribram, K. (January 1987). "A Systematic Analysis of Brain Function, Learning and Remembering." Paper presented at *Educating Tomorrow's Children* seminar. California Neuropsychology Services, San Francisco.

Rosenfield, I. (1988). *The Invention of Memory.* New York: Basic Books, Inc.

Shalley, C. (1988). *Humanities Program-Hightstown High School.* Unpublished curriculum for the integrated humanities program at Hightstown High School, Hightstown, N.J.

Springer, S., and G. Deutsch. (1985). *Left Brain, Right Brain.* New York: W.H. Freeman and Company.

Vygotsky, L.S. (1978). *Mind in Society.* Cambridge, Mass.: Harvard University Press.

The Interdisciplinary Challenge: Connection and Balance

by Richard J. Cummings

Guest Editor's note: Since Phi Kappa Phi was founded in 1897 to honor academic excellence in all of the disciplines, not just a privileged few, it is appropriate that an issue of National Forum: The Phi Kappa Phi Journal *be devoted to interdisciplinary matters. Given that Phi Kappa Phi is by definition an interdisciplinary honor society in the truest sense of the world, this issue can be regarded as a long-overdue effort to celebrate that interdisciplinary heritage.*

My journey through academic life began as a premed student with a major in biology. I discovered later, after an eighteen-month stint as a hospital corpsman in the navy, that I had serious concerns about the life-and-death responsibility that goes with medical practice and about what struck me as the dehumanizing nature of the hospital routine. To be more specific, I was acutely aware that a fatal error in diagnosis would cause me a great deal more consternation than, for instance, misquoting an important writer or thinker, and I objected to reducing patients to names, data and diagnoses on a chart. In reaction to this profoundly humanistic conflict, I began to cultivate a latent interest in language, literature, and ideas, which in turn made me conscious of the way in which we need to see one discipline in the light of others if we are to come to a full understanding of any of them.

Then after a three-and-one-half-year sojourn in Europe during which I managed to become fluent in French, Italian, Spanish, Portuguese and German, I decided to embark on an academic career, and to that end, I earned a dual doctorate at

From *National Forum: The Phi Kappa Phi Journal*, vol. 69, no. 2, p. 2-3, Spring 1989. Reprinted with permission.

Stanford University in French literature and the history of ideas. Incidentally, my study of various languages led me to agree with George Bernard Shaw who always maintained that the main reason for learning a foreign language was to come to a fuller appreciation of our native English—a concept which is closely analogous to the one about the need to acquaint others with a wide range of disciplines in order to fully grasp the one in which we choose to specialize. This emphasis on a healthy dose of generalization to complement our tendency to specialize is central to the whole concept of a liberal education. In any event, I wrote a dissertation on the problem of suffering in the works of the father of French decadence, Joris-Karl Huysmans, which had to be broad enough to satisfy both majors. Not only did I learn that it was possible to be both a specialist and a generalist at the same time, I also discovered that the two areas of involvement mutually reinforced each other: my exposure to the history of ideas provided an invaluable background for my immersion in the *fin-de-siècle* world of Huysmans.

My first year of teaching at the University of Utah was interdisciplinary in the extreme, because I had to teach courses in French language and literature, German, Italian, the history of ideas, and comparative European and American literature from 1850 to 1950. (That was an experience which I just barely survived, by the way.)

Since 1970, I have been director of the Honors Program at the University of Utah, and that has proven to be an interdisciplinarian's dream. The program has been a success largely because the outstanding faculty members who participate teach courses which deliberately cross disciplinary boundaries; faculty members team teach with others from very diverse fields, or even with nonfaculty experts from the community (in one case a class on state government was taught by a political science professor in collaboration with the governor of the state of Utah). Other successful collaborative ventures have included team teaching by a classicist and a physicist, by an English professor and a biologist, by a Russian professor and a musicologist, and by a Chinese language professor and a political scientist. Thus, we do not restrict teaching in the Honors Program to the liberal arts colleges. We draw very heavily on faculty from our professional colleges, including law, medicine, pharmacy, nursing, engineering, mines and mineral industries, and health.

Furthermore, we require students to go much further afield in completing their Honors liberal education requirements than their chosen major would imply. All nontechnical majors in the program are required to complete a full year course in the [sic] calculus and its applications to meet their Honors science requirement.

To gain perspective on the interdisciplinary challenge, we need to ask the questions, Where did the concept of the disciplines originate? and How has this history affected attempts to synthesize the disciplines? The word discipline derives from the Latin *disciplina*, which means "instruction," "training," "teaching," and "education." In the thirteenth century it came to mean "chastisement," and it was first used in the fourteenth century to mean "branch of learning." And what were the branches of learning in the middle ages? They were, of course, the liberal arts handed down from classical antiquity and codified in the trivium—grammar, rhetoric, and logic—and the "higher learning" of the quadrivium—arithmetic, geometry, astronomy, and music. But it must be remembered that at a time when the Christian church dominated all of Europe, the main "discipline" to which all the others were subservient, was theology. Now, for our purposes, two things about all of this are noteworthy.

First, there was a "ruling" discipline, namely theology, which had been raised to new heights first with marked Platonic overtones by St. Augustine and then with a strong Aristotelian undercurrent by St. Thomas Aquinas. On the other hand (and this is my second point), any scholar worth his or her salt was expected to master the other seven disciplines in toto, because the sum total of human learning was sufficiently limited that it could all be known by a single individual. This means that even though philosophy was regarded as the handmaiden of theology, the two were not really in competition, because specialized learning had not yet come into its own. Indeed, even the Renaissance with its flowering of learning produced a new breed epitomized by Leonardo da Vinci, the true "Renaissance man" who is at home in all disciplines. But then with the proliferation of learning during the subsequent centuries, specialization became more and more important, and disciplines became more and more clearly defined until, by the end of the nineteenth century, territoriality had begun to rear its ugly head.

AN UNFORTUNATE DISCIPLINARY DIFFERENTIATION: "RULING," "DROOLING," AND "DUELING" DISCIPLINES

In 1959 C.P. Snow dramatized a basic disciplinary dichotomy in his essay *The Two Cultures and the Scientific Revolution*, where he argued that, in Britain at least, science was too little understood and appreciated, especially by those in the humanities. Ironically, in the intervening decades, thanks to the great advances in science and technology, the "hard" sciences have become the "ruling" disciplines, and the social sciences, the humanities, and the fine arts have been relegated to the role of "drooling" disciplines; that is, they have been left on the sidelines longing for the ample funding and high prestige which have been lavished on the sciences. This state of affairs has led to the unfortunate spectacle of what can only be described as "dueling" disciplines, a situation in which each specialty must scramble shamelessly for its share of the pie (a pie which, admittedly, has been greatly diminished during the Reagan era of reduced appropriations for education) while ruthlessly undercutting the competition. An equally serious consequence of this cutthroat competitiveness is the way in which it seems to have shifted the focus (and even undermined the integrity) of some of what I have half-facetiously referred to as the "drooling" disciplines. I am referring to the tendency to redefine a discipline along presumably scientific, or rather pseudoscientific, lines by insisting on the need to quantify, to objectify, to reify, and ultimately to "deify" the discipline (we seem to have gone full circle back to the original ruling discipline, theology) by overstating and even sterilizing that discipline's achievements and capabilities in the name of something that masquerades as scientific validation. A quick sampling of some of the headings and offerings in a current course catalogue gives concrete evidence of what I am talking about: "Linguistics and Cognitive Science," "Military Science," "Sport Science," "Quantitative Psychology," "Technical Aspects of Commercial Recreation," and so on.

> The "hard" sciences have become the "ruling" disciplines, and the social sciences, the humanities, and the fine arts have been relegated to the role of "drooling" disciplines.

DISCIPLINARY SYNERGISM VS. TURFISM

The interdisciplinary challenge cannot be met by expecting disciplines to defer to each other any more than it can be addressed by allowing them to wall themselves off from each other. There must be a willingness to make connections wherever that is profitable and feasible, and there must also be a willingness to achieve balance within individual disciplines where old, established ideas must be revitalized and even supplanted by new and often unsettling concepts, just as there must be balance among the various fields of specialization where synergism and not turfism should light the way. This can lead to what, at first blush, may well seem to be strange bedfellows. For example, on my own campus, which has gained a certain measure of distinction thanks to the development and first successful utilization of the artificial heart, we have a Department of Bioengineering which brings together such unlikely collaborators as engineers, surgeons, materials scientists, physiologists, ophthalmologists, anaesthesiologists, pharmacists, chemists, pathologists, social workers, physicists, and radiologists (to name just a few). Disciplines obviously exist because they provide a haven within which like-minded scholars can unite to concentrate on a field of inquiry, and advance the frontiers of knowledge thanks to a highly focused joint effort. But focused effort does not mean wearing blinders and cultivating tunnel vision. It is pursued most effectively when meticulous scrutiny of a carefully delimited area of knowledge is accompanied by a breadth of vision sufficient to enable the researcher to see how his or her investigation fits into the bigger picture.

> The interdisciplinary challenge cannot be met by expecting disciplines to defer to each other any more than it can be addressed by allowing them to wall themselves off from each other. There must be a willingness to make connections wherever that is profitable and feasible.

SOME MAJOR INTERDISCIPLINARY ISSUES

The interdisciplinary challenge touches on many topics only a few of which can be addressed in the brief compass of this printing of *National Forum*. The following are some of the major issues which are touched upon in significant ways by the accompanying articles:

- Evaluating social science paradigms: How do we recognize the limits of models?
- Specialists vs. generalists: can we reconcile this apparent conflict within the context of interdisciplinarity?
- Interdisciplinary models: Does the way in which we conceptualize the thinking process influence for good or ill the kinds of products we introduce into the marketplace?
- The interdisciplinary mind-set: Does thinking in interdisciplinary terms enhance creativity and broaden understanding?
- Writing across the curriculum: How can this be enhanced by an interdisciplinary approach?
- Designing unusual interdisciplinary programs: Honors, Science, Technology, and Society, etc.
- The future of interdisciplinary studies: What lies ahead?

In addition to these issues, authors have examined promising new juxtapositions such as poetry and the computer as well as psychotherapy and the arts.

AN INTERDISCIPLINARY ROLE MODEL

Although it is neither appropriate nor feasible for me to summarize the contents of this issue, I would like to comment briefly on the article of Rollo May as a veritable paradigm of interdisciplinary writing and thinking. His title, "The Therapist and the Journey into Hell," though appropriate for his central role as a well-known psychotherapist, also immediately suggests two other disciplines—theology and literature. We sense from the title that there could well be some allusion here to Virgil and Dante, and indeed the essay makes extensive use of both of these literary figures. Then, in the first two paragraphs, May draws upon four other disciplines; economics, medicine, history, and cinematography, and he does it in a manner that is neither forced nor artificial, but is rather a spontaneous part of his own natural, organic discourse. Only in the third paragraph does he become consciously interdisciplinary when he states that "human beings need some mixture of professions." He also humanizes his discussion by pointing out how important friendship is to his own field, just as it should be to the exponents of all fields of inquiry.

Much of the remainder of the essay focuses on myth which he uses as a kind of interdisciplinary *lingua franca*, since it draws on—and unites—psychology, literature, philosophy, and sociology. He then speaks of his own general field of psychology as occupying a mediating place in culture, but later he does not hesitate to speak of the limits of therapy, thereby avoiding any tendency to place his own discipline in some hierarchically privileged position with respect to the others. He also mentions the central role of reason in his own field, but adds that the importance of intuition must not be overlooked.

Finally, Rollo May also notes that his field must deal with ethical concerns, since it regards "life as community…the freedom to love." May demonstrates almost with a vengeance how important true cultural literacy is to the full understanding and exploitation of one's own discipline and the understanding and appreciation of the other disciplines of which it is an integral part. Indeed, exponents of a discipline who are functional cultural illiterates outside their own fields are almost monstrous in their potential to wreak damage in a way that is reminiscent of Goethe's sorcerer's apprentice who unleashes powers he can neither understand nor control.

We must never lose sight of the fact that disciplines are convenient but artificial constructs: academia may be divided into disciplines, but the world is not. Just as the regime of President Gorbachev is promoting the new openness of *glasnost* in the interest of *perestroika,* a progressive restructuring of the old bureaucracy, so scholars and academics should be open to new relationships and realignments which can strengthen their understanding and effectiveness, and are bound to prove beneficial to all concerned. If recombinant DNA technology, a mindboggling product of interdisciplinary effort, offers a whole new spectrum of possibilities in the life sciences, so a dynamic move in the direction of what might be called "recombinant disciplines" could pave the way for new, undreamt-of prospects for the next century.

Curriculum Overview: What's the Big Picture?

*Two stonecutters…were engaged in similar activity. Asked what they were doing, one answered, "I'm squaring up this block of stone." The other replied, "I'm building a cathedral."—*Willis Harman, *Global Mind Change,* 1988, p. 144

What's the "big picture" concerning curriculum integration? What are the underlying questions and critical issues? What is our vision of schooling? And what role does curriculum integration play in that vision?

Consider the following analogy: *restructuring* schools is to *reconceptualizing* schooling as a *tree house* is to a *sand castle.* The tree house is created from scraps lying about; it is constructed around the existing trunk of the old tree. It is a vertical structure, usually with a single passageway that is designed to keep others out. Just so, with the *restructured* school. It uses the old traditional fragments of curriculum and instruction with existing structures and procedures; the mandates are top down; teachers work alone behind closed doors, keeping others out.

The *sand castle,* on the other hand, draws from the abundance of natural resources. It expands using ornate architectural designs in a horizontal pattern and invites others to join in. (Evidence the numbers on hands and knees, digging in at the beach site of any sand castle construction zone.) So too, is the *reconceptualization* of schooling. In the new vision, a horizontal integration of ideas is obvious; an enriched curriculum responding to the individual craftsman results. Participation by all stakeholders grows and collaborative teams work together as they create schools that promote learning for all students.

To look at the "big picture" is to reconceptualize (not re-structure) schooling with curriculum designs that are holistic, integrative, and visionary.

This section begins with a comprehensive analysis of the practical and conceptual issues regarding curriculum integration. Relan and Kimpston present a rich overview of the issues that includes historical reasons for curriculum integration, discussions of the various levels of integration described by degree or depth, and a critique of curriculum integration that looks at the structure of the disciplines and practical considerations. In the end, they "advocate systemic, conscious effort toward integration."

In a second essay, Lewis makes the case for curriculum integration as a tool for school reform. Cited among the common themes that reoccur in school reform movements are: an emphasis on thinking skills, more rigorous content for all students, influence from outside groups, and acknowledgment of the limits imposed by standardized testing. The piece concludes that, "the restructuring of education will collapse unless it is accompanied by substantive changes in what students learn." This statement is supported with specific references to the various discipline-based organizations that recommend more integration across the subject areas.

Gaff offers a piece that discusses the resurgence of interest in integrated learning. The author suggests several phases of integration, with the ultimate phase being one in which each discipline illuminates an issue or problem with equal force. He concludes with a serendipitous statement that is encouraging in terms of continued interest in integrative learning models. Gaff explains, "Surprisingly, although these programs were crafted primarily to provide better education for students, they are an important source for faculty renewal."

Finally, Beane offers a perspective from the level of a middle-school educator. In his article he addresses some questions and concerns with respect to integrated curricula. He advises practitioners to be open to conversations about curriculum and warns them against trying to "jam the concept into the categories of our present subject-centered structures."

Curriculum Integration: A Critical Analysis of Practical and Conceptual Issues

by Anju Relan and Richard Kimpston

In prevailing curriculum development practices, it is tacitly assumed that all learning must be compartmentalized into specialized macro units, or "disciplines", e.g., music, drama, mathematics, art—resulting in what is referred to as a "subject-centered" curriculum. Such an approach was a natural outcome of the necessity for specialization that followed the advent of the industrial revolution (Haas, 1975). Although it has been highly successful in fomenting economic growth, materialistic wealth, scientific and military power—discontentment with such isolated forms of disseminating knowledge has begun to emerge. Thus, "the entire conventional structure of subjects and subdivisions of knowledge...have reflected a grossly outworn, atomistic model of both the universe and the man." (Brameld, 1970, p. 346).

Historically, public education has mirrored societal vicissitudes, which is evident in present times. Declining growth rates in the American economy coupled with a failure to compete internationally has resulted in several criticisms levelled against prevailing educational practices. To enumerate a few, schools are characterized by fragmented schedules and a lack of relevance to real-life issues. Students are patently unmotivated with academics, and have failed to embody a holistic view of the world. The deteriorating situation has led curriculum reformers to believe that problems prevalent in schools today are an out-

(Paper presented at the annual meeting of the American Educational Research Association, Chicago, IL, April 1991), p. 1-12. Reprinted with permission.

come of unrealistic, outmoded curriculum structures which have failed to keep pace with rapid advances in society. Many educators suggest that deteriorating academic quality in schools today can be addressed with the help of a different, more relevant and realistic approach to curriculum development; an approach which presents a holistic view of knowledge to learners (Cummings, 1989; Gaff, 1989). This approach, known frequently as "curriculum integration" is the subject of the current paper. We intend to scrutinize the theoretical foundations of the concept of curriculum integration and its various interpretations, explore the models and schemes which operationalize it, and finally, present the reader with issues that are pertinent to the implementation of integrated curricula. The review and synthesis that follows examines the benefits as well as the constraints of a unified approach to curriculum development, with the hope that a clearer picture of the concept and the issues surrounding it emerges.

> In recent times, interest in and need for a unified approach to education has intensified.

WHY CURRICULUM INTEGRATION?
In recent times, interest in and need for a unified approach to education has intensified—an outcome of public outcry against the failing educational system in general, and the dissatisfaction experienced by practitioners from the inadequacy of a discipline-based approach in providing solutions to dynamic problems posed in the society. From a historical perspective, it is not surprising that strictures about the inadequacies of a weakening social and economic system are directed at the existing curriculum ideology. Today, the subject-focused curriculum is a target of criticism, in failing to provide learners with desirable intellectual skills needed for a competitive society. It is believed that the world is increasingly acquiring a global, interdependent outlook; provincial, parochial attitudes stultify efforts toward economic and academic progress. (Cummings, 1989; Zverev, 1977). Further, society is experiencing change at rate unprecedented in human history; there is need for curriculum to keep pace with these changes. A subject-centered curriculum is allegedly far from the realities of life, lacking in "relevance." In the

late sixties, Foshay pointed out the inadequacy of a subject-centered curriculum in dealing directly with the relationship between education and life—thus one can be thorough in the study of physics, but be completely ignorant about the problem of racial injustice, poverty.

The evolving society has implications for the changing nature of knowledge. For example, Cohen (1988) proposes that with increasing information, new disciplines emerge due to the combination of old ones, e.g., biophysics, biochemistry. She believes that students must know the process of this syntheses. A multitude of recent social and ecological disasters have exemplified that disciplinary boundaries are temporary and penetrable (Haas, 1975). In such instances, when entities or concepts are viewed from one perspective or discipline, grave repercussions are felt in other fields (for example, the use of DDT as a pesticide). Finally, the convenient but artificial compartmentalization of disciplines does not adequately represent the world, which is not made up of such artificial constructs (Cummings, 1989). Thus effort should be expended on fitting specialized viewpoints into the big picture.

Schools are constantly trying to accommodate an exponential growth of knowledge, resulting in a conflict in what should be taught, and what should be eliminated (Jacobs, 1989). Compounded with this is the assimilation of newer subjects, for example, AIDS (Acquired Immune Deficiency Syndrome) and drugs, and chemical education, adding new pressures and constraints on times allocated to subjects. Teachers and students are frustrated with fragmented schedules in schools today. Jacobs suggests that a unified approach would not only resolve these problems, but make curriculum more relevant and useful to the learner regardless of the content being taught. An integrated curriculum helps students understand a complex, interrelated world (Gaff, 1989). Tyler (1949) supports curriculum integration as a "must" to help students gain a unified view of their learning. Associated with this is the belief that problems in today's world can be solved only by whole men, not those who are anything more than a technologist, artist or pure scientist, which a "rational" study of disciplines seems to promote (Foshay, 1970).

An integrated approach is viable from a psychological perspective. Gestalt psychologists believe that entities are considered as wholes rather than individual parts—thus knowledge should be presented as a whole for easy assimilation. Advocates of the schema theory believe in the activation of links and nodes in memory for effective encoding and retention (Anderson, 1980). From this viewpoint, the greater this spread of activation, the easier it is to anchor new concepts to those existing in memory. A curriculum that is more relevant to the learner will also permit deeper levels of processing.

> With such integration, the acquisition of vital learning skills would be enhanced; and content will be more relevant to students, making them independent ... learners.

Integrating higher order *skills* across the curriculum has been gaining popularity. Ackerman and Perkins (1989) state that with such integration, the acquisition of vital learning skills would be enhanced; and content will be more relevant to students, making them independent, proactive learners. Transfer of skills would be encouraged and process and content goals would be unified.

Other arguments for an integrated approach stem from its ability to actively involve students in their own education. Because of the process-oriented approach in many forms of curriculum integration, it is assumed that students are actively involved as decision-makers and problem-solvers. Cooperative learning is fostered and different ability and interest levels are easier to accommodate (North Carolina State Dept. of Public Instruction, 1986).

Thus, hypothetically, a unified approach to curriculum offers several advantages relevant to the needs of contemporary society. At this juncture, however, the concept of an "integrated curriculum" is yet unclear, and we explicate that in the next section.

CONCEPTS AND LEVELS OF INTEGRATED CURRICULUM

What is meant by curriculum integration? Is it the fusion of two or more subjects? Is it studying one content area from the viewpoint of another? Is it content-based at all? Published work on different forms and methods of integrating curricula reveals diverse interpretations of the term, and is characterized by an abundance of alternate terminology (e.g., multidisciplinary studies, interdisciplinary, fused curriculum, correlated curriculum, transdisciplinary studies, unified studies, etc.). The plethora of terms centered around a single concept indicates the significance of certain fundamental questions in aiding an understanding of the exact nature of benefits, conceptualization and implementation of an integrated program.

Traditionally, integrated approaches to curriculum design have been associated with some form of "intermingling" of disciplines which goes beyond the compartmentalized, specialized teaching of each discipline. This form of integration is referred to variously as "multidisciplinary," "interdisciplinary," and "transdisciplinary." The focus in these approaches is on different ways of combing disciplines, so that "integration" of a desirable form is achieved.

One of the more popular forms of integrating curricula are operationalized with the help of problem-oriented approaches, in which no conscious attempt is made to study specialized disciplines.

In recent times curriculum integration has assumed an inclusive interpretation, which extends beyond a combination of disciplines. Thus included in this interpretation are the integration of across-the-domain skills such as thinking, reasoning and problem-solving capabilities (for example, Bereiter, 1986; Ackerman & Perkins, 1989), the teaching of learning strategies, and the addition of topics and subjects in the curriculum, which have not been structurally recognized as unique disciplines, for example, AIDS, drug, nutrition, and career education (the "nondisciplinary fields"). Thus unplanned forms of integration, occurring most simply at the level of combining two disciplines, as well as fully integrated programs can be considered examples of "curriculum integration."

One of the more popular forms of integrating curricula are operationalized with the help of problem-oriented approaches, in which no conscious attempt is made to study specialized disciplines. Short and Jennings (1976) advocate a "multidisciplinary" approach which is "holistic, and makes collective use of the disciplines." (p. 592). In a similar vein, Kersh, Nielson & Subotnik (1987) state that integrative curricula unify subject matter from a wide variety of disciplines around a series of generalizations. Cohen (1978) considers interdisciplinarity as "an attitude as well as a set of methods for posing problems that transcend subject matter boundaries and in fact [are] created by them." (p. 125). Jacobs (1989) defines an "interdisciplinary" curriculum as a knowledge view and curriculum approach that consciously applies methodology and language from more than one theme to examine a central theme, issue, problem, topic, or experience. Thus the "multidisciplinary" approach transcends all boundaries of traditional disciplines and is highly interactive, actively combining social and intellectual domains. Jacobs (1989) refers to this as a "transdisciplinary" approach, which is beyond the scope of disciplines.

Other forms of curriculum integration can be seen as reflecting an establishment of ties among different disciplines. Thus Tyler (1949) considers integration as the horizontal relationship of curriculum experiences. Henchey (in Short & Jennings, 1976), looks upon the "multidisciplinary" approach as a process based upon the analysis of "relationships" and establishment of "ties." According to Jacobs (1989), a "multidisciplinary" approach is the juxtaposition of several disciplines focused on one problem, with no direct attempt to integrate. In this definition, linkages between subjects are stressed.

> **Curriculum integration can be considered along a continuum, where different levels on the continuum specify the *degree* or *depth* of integration.**

Integrated approaches may occur at relatively "shallow" levels. For example, "crossdisciplinary" approaches view one discipline from the perspective of another. A "pluridisciplinary" approach is the juxtaposition of disciplines assumed to be more or less related (Jacobs, 1989). Finally, integration takes place without conscious attempts at providing linkages. Thus lessons are sequenced to correspond to lessons in the same area in other disciplines, but no connections are made across fields, only sequencing is such that students will find necessary linkages.

From the above interpretations we can conclude that curriculum integration can be considered along a continuum, where different levels on the continuum specify the *degree* or *depth* of integration. It is also dependent on the content, processes and skills involved in learning. Although there is some overlap in these frameworks, differences in comprehensiveness and organization set them apart as individual approaches. For example, Jacobs' (1989) scheme recommends six types of integrative strategies, depending on the depth of integration, Kimpston (1989), examines strategies for an interdisciplinary approach to curriculum as lying on a continuum. One extreme is the structuring of the plan around each separate discipline, which is not an integrated approach, but has well-known advantages. A second possibility is to focus two or more disciplines on a single area of content (the organizing center). This approach maintains the integrity of each discipline so that each provides a unique contribution and perspective to selected content. Third, it is possible to find common elements, concepts and processes in two or more disciplines (e.g., related natural and social sciences), and teach only these to develop an understanding of the perspective common to all the disciplines which have been "fused." Here the unique perspective of each fused discipline is lost in the process, but the power of the broader perspective is gained. This is the "fused" approach. Finally, the fourth approach termed the "eclectic" strategy, does not respect the boundaries of specific disciplines, or restrict itself to knowledge drawn from established disciplines. This is similar to the problem-oriented approach discussed earlier.

Another comprehensive scheme of curriculum integration is proposed by the North Carolina State Department of Public Instruction (1986). "Integrated learning" refers to the interrelatedness of the subject and skill areas within and across grades of a school program. Several qualitatively different integration strategies have been proposed. Thus integration can occur in the form of *content within a subject or skill area* (for instance, the integration of history and geography within social studies), as *skills within subjects* (for example, writing across the curriculum, thinking skills, communication skills, library/media and computer skills, guidance skills, etc.), *subject with subject* (where two subjects are blended together and presented as a unique elective, e.g., history and the arts, humanities, technology and history), *skills with skills* (for example, thinking skills and guidance skills). Finally, any combination of skills and subjects is integrated with other skills and subjects, which typically develops around a theme, problem, question or issue.

Included in the concept of curriculum integration are processes and skills, and those fields which do not currently possess the status of unique, recognized disciplines, for example, thinking and problem-solving skills, global, multicultural studies, the study of hunger, patterns in the world, etc. This type of integration is characterized by issues pertaining to the structure of disciplines to some extent, and by others which are indigenous to the process, skill or field being integrated. The integration of thinking skills are used here to illustrate the point.

Ackerman and Perkins (1989), have presented a detailed plan for integrating thinking and learning skills across the curriculum. It consists of a "futuristic alternative concept," in which curriculum throughout the grades has two levels: the curriculum, and the metacurriculum. The curriculum consists of substantive content and concepts, whereas the metacurriculum consists of learning skills and strategies which help students acquire content being taught in class, and develop the capacity to think and learn independently. It is integrated with the curriculum, so that skills of learning are scheduled and explicitly taught within the context of the content being taught. It is also integrated across subjects. According to these authors, thinking skills should be integrated across the curriculum on a day to day basis, and can be implicitly or explicitly taught, loosely or closely coupled with the content area, before and during the teaching of content areas. Skills and content can be doubly integrated: both within a subject and across the curriculum. As to what should be the focus of attention: skills or content, skills can be on one end of the continuum and content on the other, with numerous points between the spectrum. For example, in one arrangement, there is explicit content focus in content subjects, but skills focus in reading, remedial skills and study skills classes. Another approach is to view skills and content as objects of alternating instructional attention. Finally, skills may be completely integrated within content. Supportive of integrating skills across the curriculum, Bereiter (1984) recommends making thinking skills an already accepted instructional objective, or permeate the instructional program thoroughly with these activities.

> **Skills and content can be doubly integrated: both within a subject and across the curriculum.**

The inclusive nature of "integration" from these schemes is easily discernible. Also apparent is the considerable overlap in the strategies of integration represented in the schemes. For a comprehensive understanding of the nature of integration, both aspects of integration, depth and quality must be accounted for. What are the implications of these interpretations of these schemes? The following sections present a critique of the analysis presented so far, and in doing so, illuminate the considerations involved in transferring the theoretical framework into applied environments.

CURRICULUM INTEGRATION: A CRITIQUE

It is clear thus far that references to curriculum integration are made in general terms, without revealing precisely why and how such approaches should work. Since practically no long-term evaluations or studies systematically investigating the effects of any kind of integration exist, one is left to derive conclusions from the success stories recounted in isolated examples of spontaneous integration adopted by willing teachers. While such accounts amply demonstrate the enthusiasm generated among students, and are useful in indicating the feasibility of integrating different disciplines, missing from these accounts is an analysis of the underlying factors which caused a particular amalgamation of disciplines to succeed. It would be a worthwhile attempt to study this rich collection of anecdotal accounts to draw conclusions about the plausibility of fitting integrative practices in the overall scheme of curriculum design and implementation.

Thus, in spite of its speculated advantages, several basic questions about curriculum integration remain equivocal: Which factors are causal to the success of integration, and under which conditions? What is the role of the structure of disciplines in enhancing integration? Given the structure of disciplines, when is it feasible to integrate disciplines? Are some disciplines better than others for integration? To what depth must disciplines be integrated? What is the perspective one must impart to learners regarding the nature of integration? What are the benefits of planned integration versus spontaneous integrative practices followed informally by teachers? What are the effective means of implementing such an approach? Is adopting a problem-oriented approach which does not respect the boundaries of any discipline feasible and desirable?

The questions generated above have implications for conceptualizing the notion of integration and implementing some form of it in applied settings. However, given the intrinsically appealing arguments presented in favor of curriculum integration, it is easy to follow the bandwagon approach, which many practitioners are likely to do (Gibbons, 1979). We now examine integration from the perspective of the structure of disciplines and the constraints in adopting an integrated approach to curriculum. Finally, we offer suggestions on the process involved in implementing an integrated approach.

THE STRUCTURE OF DISCIPLINES

When integrating disciplines, it is natural that several questions should arise about the integrity of disciplines: How sacrosanct are the boundaries of a discipline with respect to integration? How feasible is it to integrate separate structures, biases, conflicts and language of disciplines? Viewpoints on the subject are varied.

> **The authors affirm that unless students have a foundation of individual concepts, it is impossible for them to see relationships.**

The sanctity of disciplines is valued by several writers. That individual disciplines have their own modes of inquiry, jargon, biases and language has been elegantly and extensively documented by Schwab (1964). According to Hughes (1978), "…the disciplines of knowledge, as we know them, are not arbitrary divisions. They are divisions which are permitted by the reality of the existential situation…. They have been tried and tested, and their value as vehicles for teaching cannot be ignored." (p. 166). Gozzer (1982) believes there can be no concept of the "international" without that of "national"; thus there can be no learning without a disciplinary framework. Heikkenin and Armstrong (1978) share Gozzer's belief, stating that the process of interdisciplinary learning is an increasingly complex sequence of relationships, which consists of learning about individual disciplines, learning to coordinate one discipline with another, and superordinating disciplines by integration. These authors affirm that unless students have a foundation of individual concepts, it is impossible for them to see relationships, or use inquiry, analysis and synthesis to explore a particular perspective. In Foshay's words (1970), "We must recognize that the integrity of the fields of inquiry—the disciplines—must be preserved, if they are to be learned. But this immediately makes it impossible in theory to combine disciplines into multidisciplines for instruction. The subjects must be taught separately, each in its own way, according to its own logic." (p. 125).

Integration is also based on certain assumptions which may be questionable. For example, Kindler (1987) questions the inclusion of art into the general curriculum. Integration assumes that there is similarity across the arts. However, sometimes focusing on one kind of art without interference from others allows more profound involvement in that art form. Arts are expressive in nature, but the expression takes very different forms in each art area e.g., the concept of rhythm in music and visual arts is very different, the meaning is different in each art medium. Kindler feels that long term integration should present numerous problems—the focus may become narrow in one or both the media. Further, each discipline has its own logical sequence, thus coordination may be difficult in both. Kindler is also concerned with transfer of artistic skills—creativity in one medium does not guarantee it in another, there may not be any transfer.

Integration of knowledge is subject-specific, that is, it depends on the nature of disciplines being integrated (Gibbons, 1979). Using an analytical approach to integrating physics and math, the author demonstrates that knowledge has coherence or synthesis within certain broad fields of experience. A different set of hypotheses is arrived at using integration of content from history and sociology, implying that one cannot make generalizations about integration, it is unique to all domains. According to Gibbons, integration of knowledge from different domains is not only possible but a normal feature of the pursuit of knowledge. However, teachers and students pursuing integrated studies must find out the nature of the domain of enquiry and the instrumental domain, as well as the nature of concepts and propositions in the two domains.

Ackerman (1989) looks at the question of integration from a more applied emphasis, enumerating the intellectual and practical criteria which should be considered in curriculum integration. Speaking for the integration of higher order thinking skills, the author believes that integration must actually enhance the learning of disciplines—students should grasp the subjects better than if they were taught separately; students must derive benefit beyond the disciplines; and finally, students may acquire flexible thinking processes in different situations, understand their limitations better, which will assist in the development personal attributes.

> In making decisions about integrating curricula, the practical criteria must not be underestimated. Of utmost importance are the attitudes and academic preparation of teachers, reactions of students, parents and community, equipment needs and new expertise.

There are grounds for conflict in the two outcomes being considered: keeping the integrity, the indigenous logic and structure of a discipline, versus "integrating" disciplines so that the boundaries among subjects no longer exist. Brameld (1970) theorizes that the structure of the curriculum may be symbolized in the form of a moving "wheel," in which the rim is the unifying theme of mankind—its predicaments and aspirations, the hub is the central question of any given period of learning, and spokes are the supporting areas of concentrated attention that bear most directly upon each respective question. In this framework, within a problem-oriented approach, individuals are allowed to develop their areas of interest and concentration. Presenting a similar viewpoint, Jacobs (1989) reiterates that one can accomplish both—teach via an interdisciplinary approach and retain the unique flavor of each discipline. However, such schemes are conjectures at this point, how effectively they can be accomplished can be ascertained only after systematic research and evaluation.

What conclusion then, is one left with regarding the structures of disciplines and their effects on integration? The answer lies in the nature of integration one is trying to accomplish. Some schemes or strategies of integration described earlier illuminate the issue. For example, Kimpston's strategies of integrating curricula considers different types of integration—those in which it is not necessary to lose the thread of inquiry found in each discipline, as well as a problem-oriented approach, in which no reference is made to the disciplines. An insightful approach for the practitioner of integration would be to study these schemes, analyze the structure of the disciplines being pooled, and select a strategy which would best enhance what is being synthesized. Failure to do so can result in what Jacobs terms the "potpourri problem," which leads to a lack of "staying power" of interdisciplinary approaches in schools; such units possess no general structure, resulting in a sampling of each of the subjects which are combined.

CURRICULUM INTEGRATION: SOME
PRACTICAL CONSIDERATIONS

In making decisions about integrating curricula, the practical criteria must not be underestimated. Of utmost importance are the attitudes and academic preparation of teachers, reactions of students, parents and community, equipment needs and new expertise (e.g., Salt, 1969).

Perhaps the most important among these is the academic and psychological preparation of teachers: Are teachers equipped to implement integrated approaches? In elementary grades, teachers often practice integration spontaneously. However, beyond elementary grades, as teachers' knowledge about disciplines becomes more specialized, instruction increasingly acquires a more subject-centered approach. It is not clear how well teachers who have been a part of subject-centered education, and have never experimented with unified approaches would react to integrated courses. As Cadenhead (1970) states, connections between disciplines can be made at several educational levels, however, the degree to which it is applied will be determined by the teacher's knowledge, attitude and expertise in various subjects and the application of the principle. Using transdisciplinary approaches requires a major shift in teaching strategies. For example, Romey (1975) acknowledges that, "A basic change in level of consciousness is required to accomplish [transdisciplinary studies]. My role as a facilitator of learning changes dramatically when I, too, enter the area of the unknown, the new problem, rather than resting comfortably back in the zone of familiar methods and concepts." (p. 33). Heikkenin and Armstrong (1976) present evidence that only teachers functioning at a highly developed conceptual understanding of science can deal adequately with the idea of a unified approach to science.

Bollen (1977) argues that teachers are specialists, and may be enthusiastic for their own subjects, not others'. Second, teaching certain subjects, e.g., sciences requires a number of equipment and safety considerations, thus it would need considerable inservice training to make teachers experts in fulfilling the safety requirements. The importance of teachers in the learning process is stressed by Hughes (1978), who believes that it is the quality of teachers which makes a difference in learning, not the curriculum per se.

Second, curriculum integration, like any aspect of curriculum, is a social process, involving parents, students, teachers, the community and administrators. The success of integrated programs would depend on the participation, consensus and understanding by all of what is to be accomplished. The decision to adopt an integrated approach would result in a different set of physical and intellectual needs, and require a restructuring of personnel; all such changes must be accounted for before launching an integrated program.

> In the existing curriculum development practices, acceptance for integrated dissemination of knowledge must penetrate more than one level of administration to have an impact.

CONCLUSION

Curriculum integration must not be considered as a random combination of disciplines, as the term may imply. Nor should it be practiced without a systematic, methodical analysis of goals, the underlying philosophy, the structure of disciplines being considered for integration, practical constraints and schemes of implementation. In this paper, we have attempted to highlight those issues involved in curriculum integration which are often overlooked in the design of such curricula. Examples can be seen in how hastily subjects pertaining to contemporary social issues are "integrated" into school curricula, without adequate foresight into their effects on already overburdened teachers, and their overall impact on students intellectually and socially. As Haas (1975) states, "In this century American education has had numerous flirtations with schemes of integrating knowledge—core curriculum, fusion, broad fields. Due primarily to the power of tradition, weak formulations of rationales, and little concern for a philosophy of knowledge, these schemes have led struggling and short existences." (p. 9).

We advocate a systematic, *conscious* effort toward integration, which is not only practiced by individual teachers themselves, but is supported by the school and district administration, as well as students and parents. We believe that in the existing curriculum development practices, acceptance for integrated dissemination of knowledge must penetrate more than one level of administration to have an impact—in making a difference in the learners' holistic conception of knowledge. In this less radical approach toward curriculum reform, we believe that a subject-based curriculum ought not to be eliminated altogether, however, relationships among disciplines must be made explicit. Disciplines which share unifying structures, e.g., sciences, should be disseminated with an integrated emphasis (Adenyl, 1987; Chapman, 1976; Showalter, 1975).

Models of integrated curricula delineated recently by Jacobs, and Ackerman and Perkins (1989) indicate a trend in which ambiguity about the nature of integration is beginning to lessen—these models outline clear conceptions and designs for curriculum integration. In spite of existing models, discretion is required before decisions regarding integration are made. Of ultimate importance are the clarity of goals for implementation—what will be accomplished through a certain type of integration? Unless there is consensus by all who will be affected by the project, at some level the attempt at integration may lose momentum and focus.

A more radical approach would be to adopt an entirely holistic approach to learning, in which students feel free to study unifying themes, problems and concepts, without being confined to any discipline. Such a philosophy, which is advocated by many theorists, would require a major restructuring of the school system at all levels. A major concern here is related to expectations of teachers—subconsciously, it would be natural to expect teachers to be subject specialists as well as effective facilitators of integrated learning. This ought to be avoided, with clear expectations delineated for teachers (Hamilton, 1973). Consensus among everyone involved in the restructuring at a philosophical and psychological level would be a major issue.

BIBLIOGRAPHY

Ackerman, D. (1989). Intellectual and practical criteria for successful curriculum integration. In Jacobs, H. (Ed.). *The interdisciplinary Curriculum, Design and Implementation*, ASCD: Alexandria, Vancouver.

Ackerman, D. and Perkins, D. N. (1989). Integrating thinking and learning skills across the curriculum. In Jacobs, H. (Ed.). *The Interdisciplinary Curriculum, Design and Implementation*, ASCD: Alexandria, Vancouver.

Adenyl, E. O. (1987). Curriculum development and the concept of "integration" in science—Some implications for general education. *Science Education, 71*, 523-533.

Anderson, J. R. (1980). *Cognitive Psychology and its implications*. San Francisco, CA: Freeman.

Bereiter, C. (1984). How to keep thinking skills from going the way of all frills. *Educational Leadership, 42*(1), 75-77.

Bollen, F. A. (1977). Does "science for all" have to be "unified science"? *Education in Science, 75*, 25-26.

Brameld, T. (1970). A cross-cutting approach to the curriculum: The moving wheel. *Phi Delta Kappan, 51*, 346-348.

Burns, R. & Brooks, G. D. (1970). The need for curriculum reform. *Educational Technology, 10*(4), 8-12.

Cadenhead, K. (1970). Needed: A plan that capitalizes on relationships among disciplines. *Elementary English, 45*(7), 988-92.

Chapman, B. (1976). The integration of science or the disintegration of science education? *School Science Review, 58*, 134-146.

Cohen, M. (1978). Whatever happened to interdisciplinary education? *Educational Leadership, 36*(2), 122-26.

Cummings, R. J. (1989). The interdisciplinary challenge: Connection and balance. *National Forum: Phi Kappa Phi Journal*, Spring, 2-3.

Foshay, A. W. (1970). How fare the disciplines? *Phi Delta Kappan, 51*, 349-52.

Gaff, J. G. (1989). The resurgence of interdisciplinary studies. *National Forum: Phi Kappa Phi Journal*, Spring, 4-5.

Gibbons, J. A. (1979). Curriculum integration. *Curriculum Inquiry, 9*, 321-332.

Gozzer, G. (1982). Interdisciplinarity: A concept still unclear. *Prospects, 12*, 281-292.

Haas, J. D. (1975). For lack of a loom: Problems in integrating knowledge. *School Science and Mathematics, 75*(1), 4-14.

Hamilton, D. (1973). The integration of knowledge: Practice and problems. *Journal of Curriculum Studies, 5*(2), 146-55.

Heikkinen, M. W. & Armstrong, T. (1978). Unified science and teacher's conceptual level. *School Science and Mathematics, 78,* 513-516.

Hughes, A. S. (1978). Separate subject and integrated approaches to social education. *History and Social Studies Teacher, 13*(3), 163-67.

Jacobs, H. (1989). The growing need for interdisciplinary discipline content. In Jacobs, H. (Ed.). *The Interdisciplinary Curriculum, Design and Implementation,* ASCD: Alexandria, Vancouver.

Kersh, M. E., Nielson, M. E. & Subotnik, R. F. (1987). Techniques and sources for developing integrative curriculum for the gifted. *Journal for the Education of the Gifted, 11*(1), 58-68.

Kindler, A. M. (1987). A review of rationale for integrated arts programs. *Studies in Art Education, 29*(1), 52-60.

Kimpston, R. D. (1989). Multidisciplinary approaches to curriculum: Some basic strategies. Unpublished manuscript, University of Minnesota.

North Carolina State Department of Public Instruction, Raleigh. Instructional Services (1987). Integrated learning—what, why and how? ERIC Document Reproduction Service No. ED 290759.

Romey, W. D. (1975). Transdisciplinary, problem-centered studies: Who is the integrator? *School Science and Mathematics, 75*(1), 30-38.

Salt, J. (1969). Problems of integrated education (1969). *Trends in Education, 16,* 23-37.

Schwab, J. (1964). *The structure of the disciplines: Meanings and significances.* Rand McNally and Co.

Short, E. C. & Jennings, T. T. Jr. (1976). Multidisciplinary: An alternative approach to curriculum thought, *Educational Leadership, 33*(8), 590-94.

Showalter, V. (1975). Rationale for an unbounded science curriculum. *School Science and Mathematics, 75*(1), 15-21.

Zverev, I. D. (1977). Pedagogical research problems of the general curriculum. *Soviet Education, 19*(8), 80-96.

Getting Unstuck: Curriculum as a Tool of Reform

by Anne C. Lewis

*In the last two years, concern about the school curriculum has pro-
duced its own subgenre of national reform reports. Ms. Lewis re-
views the reports on the core subjects and points out some common
themes.*

The nation's academic needle appears to be stuck. Despite the
efforts of more than 200 public commissions and task forces
dedicated to improving academic performance in the
schools, despite higher graduation requirements enacted in 45
states, despite consistent messages that amount to Uncle Sam
pointing at young people and saying, "I want you to think
smarter," it isn't happening.

After almost seven years of serious, wide-ranging efforts to
reform schools, students don't seem to be learning much more.
Scores on the Scholastic Aptitude Test are stagnant. Achievement trends in reading and writing, according to the latest data
from the National Assessment of Educational Progress (NAEP),
show almost straight lines for white and Hispanic students; only
black students have registered significant progress, and the gap
between the proficiency of whites and that of black and Hispanic minorities remains alarmingly large. Although American
students apparently spend nearly as much time in math class
and doing math homework as do Asian students, the dismal
performance of Americans on international assessments has become predictable. In science assessments, American students
regularly bring up the rear, competing with underdeveloped nations to stay out of last place.

The cheap, easy policy of requiring students to take more
core academic subjects passed over the nation's classrooms with

From *Phi Delta Kappan*, vol. 71, no. 7, p. 534-538, March 1990.
Reprinted with permission.

hardly a ripple. Higher requirements resulted in more students, especially middle- and low-achievers, enrolling in basic academic courses, according to William Clune and others in a study for the Center for Policy Research in Education. However, higher requirements "failed in getting students into the most rigorous possible courses, in producing a reasonably uniform education for all students, and probably, in conveying the higher-order skills necessary for a competitive economy," Clune says.[1]

It is no wonder, then, that the content of what students are studying has become the new focus of reform. The heavy hand of top-down state regulation has for the most part played itself out, and the effect of the school restructuring movement is still uneven.

Concern about what students are learning did not develop smoothly. Indeed, the first major reform report that followed the 1983 release of *A Nation at Risk* was issued by a commission of the National Science Board, and dealt with national goals for science, mathematics, and technology education. The five-year-old Coalition of Essential Schools is now a network of about 100 schools that have implemented variations on Theodore Sizer's ideas regarding an essential core curriculum. Schools using a Paideia program are also working on curricular issues. When William Bennett was secretary of education, he played with curriculum changes by developing courses for the hypothetical James Madison High School. California's massive reform movement depends essentially on curricular reform, interweaving curricular goals and guides with textbook adoptions, statewide tests, and teacher training.

However, only in the last two years has concern about the school curriculum produced its own subgenre of national reform reports. They cover the core subjects: science, mathematics, social studies, and language arts. A few wander farther afield, dealing with such subjects as agricultural literacy or school health. But, for the most part, these curriculum reports have focused on knowledge and skills considered essential. Furthermore, despite little cross-fertilization among the various commissions and report-writing teams, the analyses of curriculum reforms are producing some common themes.

• *Integration of curricula.* This takes several forms. There are the writing and reading-across-the-curriculum efforts.

Alignment proposals—integrating texts, teacher's manuals, and assessments—have already been enacted in a few states, notably in California. And interdisciplinary teaching, which is becoming more and more popular in secondary schools, is endorsed in many of the curriculum studies. (Some critics of the social studies curriculum, who see the study as a desirable substitute for their studies, have demurred.) An overall view of the NAEP results, published a year ago by the Educational Testing Service, described one aspect of the problem of curriculum integration as the "layer cake" phenomenon. In many cases, the

> **The curriculum is treated as a collection of discrete content areas in which teachers move from one topic to another in lockstep fashion.**

report said, "the curriculum is treated as a collection of discrete content areas in which teachers move from one topic to another in lockstep fashion. As a result, lessons are often developed in isolation from one another and fail to help students relate their new learnings to what they already know."[2]

 • *Emphasis on thinking skills.* The NAEP reports have been consistent in their findings about the inability of students to go beyond basic skills—their inability to elaborate, to synthesize, and to solve problems. While this failing is certainly related to uncreative instructional strategies, dull content is considered equally at fault. The pattern begins with the minimalism of basal readers, say the curriculum reports, and continues through secondary texts and the minimum competency testing that emphasizes discrete, unelaborated skills.

 • *More rigorous content for all students.* The content of remedial programs has come under fire, with critics contending that students in these programs are doubly burdened by repetitious, dull content and by instructional strategies that do not match their learning styles. Clune's study also found that, since the reforms, courses with minimal academic content have taken the place of more helpful vocational courses for a large number of middle- or low-achieving students—thus putting these students at an even greater disadvantage.

 • *Influence of outside groups.* A common trait of the curriculum reform movement is the influence exercised by "outside" groups. With the exception of the language arts, much of the impetus for change in the curricula of various disciplines has come from outside the professional education community. For example, the National Geographic Society has pushed reforms in geography education, and the National Science Foundation is funding initiatives in math and science. (The latter two subjects were the only curriculum-related topics on the standard-setting agenda of the National Governors' Association and the White House.) Meanwhile, the National Endowment for the Humanities continues to push for curriculum reform in areas of its interest.

> It is becoming obvious that society wants a different product from its schools.

While it is true that few education agencies have sufficient resources to fund research on the curriculum, some states—especially California and New York—have demonstrated that the education community can mount major changes in instructional content (if it can muster the will). Yet the pressure to change from the outside doesn't surprise Frances Haley, executive director of the National Council for the Social Studies. The school curriculum reflects society, she points out, "and it is becoming obvious that society wants a different product from its schools."

• *Acknowledgment of the limits imposed by standardized testing.* On this subject, educators are taking the lead. Curriculum reformers "keep running into barriers created by standardized testing," notes David Florio, formerly with the National Science Foundation and now a legislative aide to Christopher Cross, the new assistant secretary for research and improvement in the U.S. Department of Education. "High-stakes tests," the norm-referenced and commercially produced standardized tests, are text-imbedded and truly "set the whole style of learning," Florio says. In his view, one of the most encouraging aspects of current efforts to reform the curriculum is the attempt to change the nature of student assessment.

Several years ago, when Sizer suggested that exhibitions of student work offered a viable alternative to reliance on test scores, he was almost alone in challenging the numbers game imposed by standardized tests. (However, the North Dakota Study Group, under the leadership of Vita Perrone, now of Harvard University, started 20 years ago as a group opposed to standardized tests.) Today, several states and school districts are experimenting with assessments that emphasize higher-order skills. While the NAEP is not considered a "high-stakes" test, its use of different assessment techniques could serve a symbolic role and help free the curriculum from the vise of narrowly conceived tests, says Florio.

The national curriculum reports do not cover everything happening in the various fields. However, they offer some assurance of continued interest in the topic, and they provide a focal point for discussion. With so many commentaries and recommendations being released at the same time, there may be some risk of diffused energy. But these reports also reflect a growing consensus that the restructuring of education will collapse unless it is accompanied by substantive changes in what students learn.

READING/LANGUAGE ARTS

Children's lock-step progress through the curriculum of American public schools begins with basal readers. English teachers have been uncomfortable with the dominance of basal readers for a long time. But not until a January 1988 report from the National Council of Teachers of English, *Report Card on Basal Readers*, was the influence of basals openly challenged. That report was one piece of a growing movement to embrace whole-language instruction, which is the antithesis of the basal reader's emphasis on discrete skills—and of standardized testing keyed to those skills. Another important ingredient in the new look of the language arts is the quality and amount of literature stressed in classrooms, even at very early ages. Moreover, teachers are being encouraged to focus on the processes of reading and writing, which rely on integrated skills.

In the summer of 1987, an unusual three-week workshop brought together leaders in the field of English education to hammer out the first major reform statement in 20 years. The English Coalition Report, *Democracy Through Language*, [3] responded to some school reforms that had narrowed the curriculum and constricted instruction. "The last thing American education needs is one more collection of inert information… to be poured raw into minds not actively engaged in reading, thinking, writing, and talking," commented Wayne Booth of the University of Chicago. Teachers should be "coaches," the report says, not dispensers of information and judges of right answers. Students should be actively engaged in learning through constant use of language in meaningful ways.

The recommendations call for fuller integration of oral language, writing, and literature, and they prefer literature over basal readers. They would eliminate tracking by ability, and they downplay mass testing in favor of consistent assessments by classroom teachers.

MATHEMATICS

The importance of problem solving and its place in the sequence of mathematics courses seems to lie at the heart of the problems with math education in the U.S. According to a series of reports, the solution is to encourage students to "think mathematically" rather than to learn by rote. Moreover, mathematics education in the U.S. remains arithmetic-based for too long. Says a commentary from the Ford Foundation:

> [The] mathematics taught in school bears little resemblance to what mathematics really is, namely a way of making sense of the world—of perceiving patterns, analyzing data, and reasoning carefully. By and large, the mathematics taught in schools is arithmetic that has been stripped of its connections to intrinsically interesting problems and ideas and reduced to a series of computational tasks with only one correct approach.[4]

While a variety of demonstrations based on good research are being conducted under the auspices of a number of universities (e.g., University of Chicago, University of California at Berkeley, University of Pittsburgh), two major reports set the tone for a new look at math education. Both deal with the curriculum. However, one is directed more at the general public; the other, more at the profession.

Everybody Counts: A Report to the Nation on the Future of Mathematics Education, by the National Research Council, sets forth recommendations for a national consensus on changes in math education. Its tone is alarmist, pointing out that three-fourths of American students stop studying math before they have finished high school—even though the demands of the current and future workplace are for more sophisticated math skills.

Everybody Counts criticizes the excessive emphasis on the mechanics of mathematics. "A mathematics curriculum that emphasizes computation and rules is like a writing curriculum that emphasizes grammar and spelling," it says. "Both put the cart before the horse."[5] Further, current instruction is too tightly tied to texts and tests. For elementary grades, the report recommends a shift from striving solely for accuracy in calculation to an effort to develop students' "number sense," which includes common sense about how to find an answer and how to choose a method. The report also supports the intelligent use of calculators in elementary school.

At the secondary level, the report recommends that all students study a common core of "broadly useful mathematics" rather than the current practice of preparing students for college calculus. Instead of tracking students, school math should provide for all students a core of "mainstream mathematics" in which different student groups are distinguished not by curricular goals but by speed, depth, and approach. What secondary students need to acquire, according to the report, is not so much a separate subject, such as algebra, but "symbol sense." College-bound students need more, of course. But rather than simply adding separate courses to their college programs, the report recommends that formal instruction in math be more integrated. Nonetheless, "all students should study mathematics every year they are in school," the report says.

Curriculum and Evaluation Standards for School Mathematics, also published in 1989, was the product of a two-year study by a commission of the National Council of Teachers of Mathematics. It sets goals for reforming K-12 math instruction, which have been endorsed by a wide range of education and other professional groups.

Each standard is grounded in the fact that students know math by doing it. "We do not assert that informational knowledge has no value, only that its value lies in the extent to which it is useful in the course of some purposeful activity," says the commission.[6] The report also notes that some quantitative techniques are needed in almost every field, not just in engineering and the physical sciences. Therefore, the commission recommends that all students be given opportunities to develop understanding of "mathematical models, structures, and simulations applicable to many disciplines." The report also argues that calculators should be available to all students at all times and that computers should be available in every classroom.

As much as possible, math knowledge should be developed from experience with problems, not taught in isolation before a student has a need for the knowledge, the report continues. In addition, students should work individually and in groups on real problems. "Learning should be guided by the search to answer questions," the report concludes.

SCIENCE

As in language arts and mathematics, traditional boundaries between subject-matter categories are apparently being blurred in science instruction. Project 2061 (named for the next year in which Halley's comet comes around) of the American Association for the Advancement of Science (AAAS) emphasizes connections across the sciences. It also stresses ideas and thinking over the rote learning of a specialized vocabulary and the memorization of isolated facts.

> As in language arts and mathematics, traditional boundaries between subject-matter categories are apparently being blurred in science instruction.

Released in 1989 by an AAAS Council on Science and Technology Education, *Science for All Americans*, the report of the first of three phases of Project 2061, defined the scientific literacy that should be acquired by all students to include:

• being familiar with the natural world and recognizing both its diversity and unity;

• understanding key concepts and principles of science;

• being aware of some of the important ways in which science, mathematics, and technology depend on one another;

• knowing that science, mathematics, and technology are human enterprises and knowing what that implies about their strengths and limitations;

• having a capacity for scientific ways of thinking; and

• using scientific knowledge and ways of thinking for individual and social purposes.[7]

The science curriculum in schools today cannot meet these goals, says the AAAS report. It must be changed, the report says, "to reduce the sheer amount of material covered; to weaken or eliminate rigid disciplinary boundaries; to pay more attention to the connections among science, mathematics, and technology; to present the scientific endeavor as a social enterprise that influences—and is influenced by—human thought and action; and to foster scientific ways of thinking."[8]

The second phase of Project 2061, now under way, is working to develop several alternative curriculum models for school districts and states. The third phase will move the reform of science, mathematics, and technology education, as envisioned by the AAAS report, to the level of the entire education system.

Meanwhile, the National Center for Improving Science Education has been working on specific curricular reforms that parallel many of those suggested in the AAAS report. The National Center's report on elementary science,[9] for example, says that science in elementary school should be given equal billing with reading, math, and writing. Furthermore, science instruction in the elementary grades should focus on fewer topics in more depth and on the skills needed for investigating and solving problems.

Likewise, the National Science Teachers Association (NSTA), in a report also published in 1989, called for greater coordination among high school science courses. Typical courses in high schools, says Bill Aldridge, executive director of NSTA, "are not coordinated, are highly abstract and theoretical, do not spend enough time on each subject, and do not use correct pedagogy. In short, we never give students the chance to understand science."[10]

The NSTA report, *Essential Changes in Secondary Science: Scope, Sequence, and Coordination*,[11] would begin formal, integrated scientific study in the seventh grade, with an emphasis on description of phenomena. More abstract concepts would be saved for later years in high school.

SOCIAL STUDIES

History and geography are the core subjects that come under the umbrella of the social studies. These subjects have also come under fire from critics for several years, and the criticisms have been reinforced by surveys indicating truly serious gaps in students' knowledge. As is the case with regard to the other major school subjects, however, reform of the social studies brings up old debates about skills versus knowledge, about specifics versus coherence among the many areas of social studies. Undoubtedly, much of the criticism springs from scholars—such as Diane Ravitch of Teachers College, Columbia University, and

Paul Gagnon of the University of Massachusetts, Boston—who believe that history has lost its central place in the social studies curriculum. A report from the Bradley Commission reinforced their views.

Another stream of criticism—most strongly expressed by Lynne Cheney, chairman of the National Endowment for the Humanities—faults the teaching of history and literature for their stress on skills. The lack of attention to content, Cheney said in *American Memory: A Report on the Humanities in the Nation's Public Schools*, produces students who have real gaps in their knowledge.[12] Social studies textbooks for the early grades, she pointed out, contain almost no history. They concentrate instead on human relations skills and life skills. High school texts are full of facts but often offer little narrative material to engage students.

> History and geography are the central subjects in the social studies, the report says. But it also retains the term *social studies* to recognize the multidisciplinary nature of the content.

The newest curriculum report in the social studies will probably be the most controversial, at least partly because the social studies are often judged more subjectively than other curriculum areas. *Charting a Course: Social Studies for the 21st Century* answers some of the criticisms of the field by recommending that the social studies focus on fewer topics in greater depth. It was produced by the National Commission on Social Studies in the Schools, which represents a broad coalition of the National Council for the Social Studies, the Carnegie Foundation for the Advancement of Teaching, and organizations of historians.

History and geography are the central subjects in the social studies, the report says. But it also retains the term *social studies* to recognize the multidisciplinary nature of the content. The working definition used by the curriculum task force said that the social studies include "history, geography, government and civics, economics, anthropology, sociology and psychology, as well as subject matter drawn from the humanities— religion, literature, and the arts"—and that social studies "combines those fields and uses them in a direct way to develop a 'systematic and interrelated study of people in societies, past and present.'"[13]

Among other recommendations, *Charting a Course* stressed that the social studies curriculum should instill "a clear understanding of the roles of citizens in a democracy" and provide opportunities to practice citizenship. It should be consistent and cumulative from kindergarten through grade 12. It should use history and geography as its matrix, emphasize critical thinking and the use of knowledge to shape individual actions, and help students critically evaluate sources.

One recommendation is sure to provoke debate. "*Selective studies of the history, geography, government, and economic systems of the major civilizations and societies should together receive attention at least equal to the study of the history, geography, government, economics, and society of the United States*," it says. "A curriculum that focuses on only one or two major civilizations or geographic areas while ignoring the others is neither adequate nor complete."[14] In some quarters, those are fighting words.

NOTES

1. William H. Clune, with Paula White and Janice Patterson. *The Implementation and Effects of High School Graduation Requirements: First Steps Toward Curricular Reform* (New Brunswick, N.J.: Center for Policy Research in Education, Rutgers University, 1989), p. 47.

2. Arthur N. Applebee, Judith A. Langer, and Ina V. S. Mullis, *Crossroads in American Education* (Princeton, N.J.: National Assessment of Educational Progress and Educational Testing Service, 1989), p. 33.

3. Richard Lloyd-Jones and Andrea Lunsford, eds., *The English Coalition Conference: Democracy Through Language* (Urbana, Ill.: National Council of Teachers of English, March 1989).

4. "QUASAR," *Ford Foundation Letter*, vol. 20, no. 3, November 1989, p. 2.

5. *Everybody Counts: A Report to the Nation on the Future of Mathematics Education* (Washington, D.C.: National Academy Press, 1989), p. 44.

6. Commission on Standards for School Mathematics, *Curriculum and Evaluation Standards for School Mathematics* (Reston, Va.: National Council of Teachers of Mathematics, 1989). p. 7.

7. *Science for All Americans: Summary* (Washington, D.C.: American Association for the Advancement of Science, January 1989), p. 4.

8. Ibid., p. 10.

9. *The Reform of Science Education in Elementary School* (Washington, D.C.: National Center for Improving Science Education, 1989).

10. Interview in *Your Public Schools* (newsletter of the Office of the Superintendent for Public Instruction, Olympia, Wash.), June 1989, p. 6.

11. *Essential Changes in Secondary Science: Scope, Sequence, and Coordination* (Washington, D.C.: National Science Teachers Association, 1989).

12. Lynne Cheney, *American Memory: A Report on the Humanities in the Nation's Public Schools* (Washington, D.C.: National Endowment for the Humanities, 1987).

13. *Charting a Course: Social Studies for the 21st Century* (Washington, D.C.: National Commission on Social Studies in the Schools, 1989), p. 3.
14. Ibid.

The Resurgence of Interdisciplinary Studies

by Jerry G. Gaff

The influence of the academic discipline is pervasive. Ever since the academy discovered the concept of disciplinary specialization around the turn of the 20th Century, disciplines have been used as the primary means for conducting the business of education. Colleges are organized by departments consisting of separate discipline; faculty are trained, hired, and promoted by colleagues within their academic discipline; the identity of college faculty as well as their professional development and their career paths are provided by their disciplinary guilds and national associations; and students are expected to specialize in a discipline as well as to sample from other specializations in order to graduate from college. For nearly a century the academic discipline has proven to be a useful device for scholars whose purpose is to acquire and transmit knowledge. The academic discipline has also served as an efficient bureaucratic device for organizing academic life.

> We are witnessing a resurgence of interest in interdisciplinary studies to correct the problems inherent in the disciplinary approach.

But academic disciplines create barriers that work against the very intellectual purposes their creators sought to advance, and periodically concerted efforts are made to overcome them. Today we are witnessing a resurgence of interest in interdisciplinary studies to correct the problems inherent in the disciplinary approach. The intellectual argument for interdisciplinary studies is that ideas from any field are enriched by theories, con-

From *The Phi Kappa Phi Journal*, vol. 69, no. 2, p. 4-5, Spring 1989. Reprinted with permission.

cepts, and knowledge from other fields. Problems of the world are not organized according to the categories of scholars; solutions to problems as diverse as pollution, defense, communications, and health require knowledge and perspectives from several disciplines. Indeed, many of the most exciting contemporary developments cross the lines of traditional disciplines: thus we have hybrid fields such as genetic engineering, cognitive sciences, and linguistics. Given the competitive climate around the globe, it is essential that we draw from all the intellectual resources of every field to improve productivity and to attack the scourges of the human community—illness, poverty, hunger, injustice, war.

> **Psychologists know that students learn better when knowledge is organized into meaningful wholes rather than isolated bits.**

The pedagogical argument for interdisciplinary studies has particular force today. The national debate which emerged during the past decade has highlighted the need for excellence in education, and several national reports have called for greater coherence in undergraduate education. The fragmentation of the curriculum with students' studying a smattering of academic disciplines, usually at an introductory level, is not sufficient. Psychologists know that students learn better when knowledge is organized into meaningful wholes rather than isolated bits. As Harlan Cleveland (author of a number of thoughtful analyses of contemporary problems in higher education) reminds us, integration is what is higher about higher education.

There is also a social argument. Learning is an individual but not solitary activity; it is more effective when it takes place within a supportive community of learning. An opportunity for all students to have a common learning experience helps to create a learning community that includes the classroom but extends beyond it. When all students study the same subjects, they have a basis for conversation outside of class about intellectual issues beyond athletics, dating, or "General Hospital." One of the prerequisites for such common learning is that the subjects covered be broader than those taught in an academic discipline so that course content engages the interests of a wide diversity of individuals. This prerequisite could be met by a set of classic texts or a series of interdisciplinary topics. By emphasizing common intellectual, cultural, or social issues, we can restore balance with the more traditional emphasis on individualism and diversity in the curriculum.

The resurgence of interest in interdisciplinary studies is more than idle talk. The national debate about quality in undergraduate education has fueled a curriculum reform movement that is producing a great number of changes on the nation's campuses. The primary focus of the reform is the general education portion of the curriculum, those courses that are required of all students for graduation. Hundreds of individual colleges and universities have taken concrete steps to strengthen their curricula, especially general education. These include all types of institutions; four-year and two-year; public and private; predominantly baccalaureate colleges and research universities; coed and single sex; and colleges located in all parts of the country. Surveys indicate that the majority of colleges and universities have made, or are in the process of making, reforms in their general education curricula. It is the rare institution of higher learning that has not been affected by the reform movement of the last decade.

The present climate of reform creates a very different dynamic for interdisciplinary studies than the dynamics present during the last period of their resurgence during the late 1960s and early 70s. At that time the interdisciplinary emphasis focused on such courses as women's studies, ethnic studies, urban studies, and environmental studies. A number of cluster colleges were created within larger institutions to provide opportunities for small groups of students and faculty to pursue their interests in these and similar types of programs. Typically these programs were small, involved a limited portion of the faculty and student body, and were relegated to the periphery of the institution. Although the programs were often powerful educationally, they were weak politically. As a consequence, many were eliminated or curtailed during the tough economic times of the late 1970s and 80s.

> **The present climate of reform creates a very different dynamic for interdisciplinary studies than the dynamics present during the last period of the resurgence during the late 1960s and early 70s.**

Today there is a concern for a higher quality education for all students, and the curricular reforms are taking place in the core of undergraduate education. New, more rigorous graduation requirements are being established. Reforms are designed to enable students to enhance their skills (including writing, speaking, foreign language, critical thinking, mathematics, and computer skills); learn about Western heritage, literature, and culture; understand cultures outside the Western tradition; become familiar with a variety of liberal arts disciplines (even if they are specializing in one of the professional fields); and acquire sensitivity to their own values and those of others. Given this driving force behind academic reforms today, interdisciplinary studies are now becoming a part of the mainstream; a requirement for all students and obligatory teaching assignment for large numbers of faculty. The new interdisciplinary structures include topical freshman seminars; required core courses in the humanities, natural sciences and social sciences; advanced courses dealing with social problems or intellectual themes; and senior projects involving original research, seminars, or artistic productions.

> **Although interdisciplinary studies have been in the ascendancy in the general education portion of the curriculum, there is reason to think that in the future they may gain a greater role within the academic major, the very citadel of specialization within institutions of higher learning.**

Although interdisciplinary studies have been in the ascendancy in the general education portion of the curriculum, there is reason to think that in the future they may gain a greater role within the academic major, the very citadel of specialization within institutions of higher learning. Ideally, a major should give students understanding of a subject in depth and also put that subject into perspective. Ernest Boyer suggests that students should acquire that perspective in an "enriched major" that requires them to examine three questions: a) What is the history and tradition of the field? b) What are the social and economic implications to be pursued? c) What are the ethical and moral issues within the specialty that need to be confronted? He says, "Rather than divide the undergraduate experience into separate camps—general versus specialized education—the curriculum at a college of quality will bring the two together." If this suggestion is taken seriously, we may see the development of a new direction for interdisciplinary studies. Academic disciplines will reach out to fields such as history, philosophy, sociology, anthropology, religion, literature, and others to design enriched majors.

For interdisciplinary courses or programs to be effective, more is needed than simply designing and legislating them. Faculty members need to reorient their thinking and develop new instructional approaches. Almost all faculty are products of a disciplinary system, and even those who are sympathetic require some assistance in removing the blinders of their specializations so they can take in new ideas, concepts, and perspectives from other fields. Faculty development, in short, is an indispensable part of successful interdisciplinary courses and programs.

A three-stage progression can be observed in the development of true integrative study. Many interdisciplinary programs start by being taught by faculty members from different fields who appear sequentially in courses; this approach constitutes a multiplicity of disciplinary perspectives without providing much in the way of conceptual integration. Whatever integration of knowledge occurs is left entirely to the students. A second stage in the development of interdisciplinary studies occurs when faculty members not only hear the lectures of their colleagues but, just as in learning a foreign language, translate the unfamiliar ideas from diverse disciplines into their own frames of reference. Faculty are still thinking in their disciplinary categories, but their boundaries have become somewhat permeable. The final stage of true integration occurs when faculty are able to perceive that other disciplines have an integrity of their own. At this stage, we realize that each discipline can illuminate an issue or problem with equal force; none is necessarily more important than another. It is this stage that Jonathan Smith, former Dean of the College at Chicago, had in mind with his Iron Law: "Students shall not be expected to integrate anything that the faculty can't or won't."

> **Students shall not be expected to integrate anything that the faculty can't or won't.**

One of the best techniques of faculty development for interdisciplinary studies programs is team teaching. Faculty members may start by searching for common intellectual interests informally or in the context of a formal seminar program and begin to design and teach a course together. Often these courses are a bit problematic to develop since the faculty have different styles and values; sometimes there is a clash over professorial authority; and students are often confused by differences of opinion among the teachers. But if faculty stick it out and work through the three-stage process noted above, they can develop exciting courses. The biggest problem with team teaching is the practical one of economics; two teachers are twice as expensive as one. One of the ways to get the benefit of collaboration without the added expense of team teaching is team planning of the program. In a workshop or seminar, faculty together work out the ideas and guidelines of courses. After one or two experiences with team teaching a course, the individuals often can teach on their own a quality interdisciplinary course that fits into the framework of the larger program.

At their best, interdisciplinary programs go beyond intellectual integration (as important as that is) to create a community of learning among students and faculty. The topics chosen for study often touch the lives of participants and foster more involvement in the process of learning. In turn, this fosters greater learning, more feedback, greater satisfaction, and group norms more supportive of intellectual inquiry. Examples of programs where these outcomes are found include the core curriculum at Brooklyn College, Western College at Miami University, the Integrative Study Program at Pacific Lutheran University, the Federated Learning Communities at SUNY-Stony Brook, and Paracollege at St. Olaf College. Surprisingly, although these programs were crafted primarily to provide a better education for students they are an important source of renewal for faculty. And although they are designed to be effective settings for teaching and learning, they also tend to stimulate interdisciplinary scholarship among faculty whose minds are stretched by their colleagues and students.

So once again we are witnessing renewed interest in interdisciplinary studies. This period of reform is producing different approaches than were present in earlier times. Although the academic disciplines continue to reign supreme in the academy, new approaches are providing an important corrective to their limited and fragmented perspectives. And because they tend to be located in the mainstream as graduation requirements for all students, rather than peripheral activities, interdisciplinary study offerings today may have greater staying power than previous ones.

Problems and Possibilities for an Integrative Curriculum

by James A. Beane

Without a doubt the second most exciting and important development in middle schools over the past few years has been the emergence of a long overdue conversation about what ought to be the middle school curriculum. The one more exciting and important development has been the reports from teachers around the country who are experimenting with new curriculum views or who are coming out from behind closed classroom doors to enlighten the rest of us about their long years of progressive teaching.

I believe that it would not be presumptuous to say that both the reports and the conversation have begun to show a pattern. That is, there is an emerging curriculum vision that goes beyond the subject-centered and multi-disciplinary approaches that have so long characterized both the junior high schools and the more recent middle schools. This newer vision has both brought to life and added to a longstanding idea that has gone by many names, and which we now refer to as an "integrative curriculum." In this paper I want to address some of the practical issues that have arisen around this idea in both conversations and classrooms. Before doing so however, we will need to look briefly back at what is meant by an integrative curriculum (Hopkins, 1937; Dressel, 1958; Beane, 1990a, 1990b, 1991, 1992).

> **An integrative curriculum works off the idea that genuine learning occurs as people "integrate" experiences and insights into their scheme of meanings.**

From *Middle School Journal*, vol. 25, no. 1, p. 18-23, September 1993. Reprinted with permission.

An integrative curriculum works off the idea that genuine learning occurs as people "integrate" experiences and insights into their scheme of meanings. Moreover, the most significant experiences are those tied to exploring questions and concerns people have about themselves and their world. Thus an integrative curriculum begins with those questions and concerns and brings to bear upon them pertinent knowledge and skill. Through the integrative and continuing process of action, interaction, and reflection, people have the possibility of constructing meanings in response to their questions and concerns. This is, of course, closely aligned with what is today called a "constructivist" approach.

> Integrative curriculum dissolves and transcends subject area lines, though it does not abandon all of the knowledge and skill that have traditionally been defined within disciplines of knowledge.

As a curriculum theory, then, integration involves more than its popular conception of simply connecting two or more subject areas while still generally maintaining their identities. Instead the integrative curriculum dissolves and transcends subject area lines, though it does not abandon all of the knowledge and skill that have traditionally been defined within disciplines of knowledge. Moreover, we have learned enough from teachers who have recently experimented with this idea to know that it opens possibilities for knowledge and skills that have often been left on the edges of the curriculum because they do not fit nicely into the ways in which the subjects have been defined in school practice. I refer here to elusive ideas like problem solving, critical analysis, ethics, valuing, question posing, and so on.

Thus we may see the present movement as away from the traditional subject area approach toward one that works with an integrated view of knowledge in the context of questions and concerns that are identified in collaboration with young people (Brodhagen, Weilbacher, & Beane, 1992). In defining ourselves in this way, however, we must heed Dewey's (1938) warning about building new theories simply out of opposition to old ones. I feel confident that the emerging theory we are working with can stand on its own since it presents a distinct case with regard to sources of the curriculum, uses of knowledge, subject-transcendent themes, and so on. Moreover, I am convinced from hearing reports from places like Kansas, Florida, Missouri, New Hampshire, Arizona, Oregon, and Wisconsin, and from reading the stories from Vermont (Stevenson & Carr, 1993) that we are on to something here. This is not just another idea that might or might not work.

Yet, in meeting with teachers and administrators in various places I am just as convinced that we have a lot of questions to consider as we try to make progress in our middle school curriculum work. Not the least of these is to more clearly and widely articulate the "why" of what we are proposing and doing. Already I am getting the feeling that people are wanting to plunge into implementation issues ("How do we do this?") when I am not sure they are clear as to why and, just as importantly, what "it" is that we are doing. I think it is very dangerous to have these discussions about how to do something before there is a clear sense of what that something is.

Now this is particularly problematic because most of us who have been involved in this conversation have tried to portray a kind of parallel structure. That is, we are trying articulate philosophy of the middle school curriculum and to sketch out a broad theory of curriculum organization. Meanwhile, while we have been willing to tell stories out of classrooms, we have carefully avoided saying exactly how that philosophy and theory ought to look in practice, that is, to give a "recipe." The parallel structure, then, amounts on the one side to a broad general statement of consistent philosophy and on the other to the need for people in local places to create many and diverse ways of bringing that philosophy to life. Thus, when asked how to actually do this, we not only should not answer (short of telling diverse stories) but cannot, since the question can only be answered in local classrooms we are not part of.

Having said this and knowing that there are now several sources people can turn to for general information about what an integrative curriculum is (e.g., Beane, 1990a; Brodhagen, Weilbacher, & Beane, 1992; Stevenson & Carr, 1993), I want to turn to some practical issues that have emerged and try to situate them in the context of this curriculum view and the changes it implies. In particular, I want to concentrate on the place of content and skills in an integrative approach.

SUBJECT MATTER IN AN INTEGRATIVE CURRICULUM

Clearly the most vexing issue for many of those engaged in the current curriculum conversation is the fate of content and skills ordinarily associated with the disciplines of knowledge as we pursue an integrative approach. I have argued repeatedly that the concept of curriculum integration does not ignore or abandon subject matter or skills but rather repositions them in the context of significant personal-social themes. Here I want to say more about that idea and identify some examples from various disciplines of knowledge and subject areas.

First, it is important to recognize that the information and skills now identified within the boundaries of disciplines of knowledge and subject areas include much, even most, of what we know about ourselves and our world, as well as ways of constructing meanings and communicating with each other. For that reason, it would be irresponsible to suggest an outright rejection of that information and skills. *But of course this was never the point of the integrative approach since it does not ask whether there should be subject matter or skills but rather how those are brought into the lives of young people and used by them.*

Perhaps it might be helpful to name some of the themes that young people have identified as we have planned with them in several situations. Recurring themes have included "Living in the Future," "Careers, Jobs, and Money," "Conflict," "Environmental Problems," and "Sex, Health, and Genetics." Within any of these, young people have numerous questions regarding their personal interests and concerns about the larger world. In order to answer these questions it is necessary to find and acquire information and to construct information-loaded meanings. Both in turn require skills of various kinds, including many that are presently promoted in schools as well as others that are more often talked about than acted upon (valuing, evaluating, critical analysis, problem solving, question posing, etc.).

The area of mathematics offers an excellent illustration of this idea. As young people conduct inquiries regarding questions about the future, they encounter numerous statistics in trend data and forecasts. To work fully with these involves an understanding of percentages, proportions, fraction, ratios, graphs, charts, and the like. To portray their own analyses and projections requires not only an understanding of how such mathematical representations are constructed, but skill in actually doing them. So it is that what is ordinarily considered to reside within the area of mathematics is not lost in an integrative curriculum; instead it takes on new and more vibrant meaning in the context of a particular theme and the related personal-social questions.

But beyond this there is the question of what happens to that part of some middle school mathematics programs that do not so obviously relate to the kinds of questions and concerns raised in an integrative curriculum. To be blunt about this, using mathematics again, what happens to pre-algebra and algebra? To respond to this concern, we must turn back to the larger middle school curriculum question and remember the concept of general education. If we define the latter as having to do with the common or widely shared concerns of young people and the larger world and if we regard such general education as the appropriate purpose of the middle school, then we must ask whether such areas of mathematics have a place in the middle school curriculum. In other words, if we commit ourselves to the idea of an integrative curriculum, then the knowledge and skill involved in the curriculum would be that, and perhaps only that, which is clearly pertinent to the particular themes, questions, and concerns that arise.

> What is ordinarily considered to reside within the area of mathematics is not lost in an integrative curriculum; instead it takes on new and more vibrant meaning in the context of a particular theme and the related personal-social questions.

This same line of thinking may now be applied to any of the other subject areas that have traditionally had a distinct place in the curriculum. Social studies, for example, would be viewed as a source of information about issues and events that might inform the social and historical meanings we construct about ourselves and our world as well as various processes for gathering and analyzing data to understand and communicate those meanings. The subject matters of science, home economics, art, music, industrial arts, and so on would be viewed similarly. Language arts would offer not only particular kinds of information, but especially possibilities of communicating meanings. And in all of these, the questions remain of how these arise in an integrative curriculum and whether all that is currently done within them would survive scrutiny as to its pertinence in an integrative approach to general education.

It would be a mistake to underestimate the significance of this issue because responding to it involves not only so-called "curriculum" thinking, but political issues as well (as if the two are ever separate). Also, for those of us who do workshops on possibilities of dissolving subject area lines this question is also hard not to notice since it comes up so frequently—sometimes before we even get started. In an effort to reduce tension and apprehension, the content retention question is often answered, "Don't worry, what you have always taught will still be there." I want to suggest here that such a response is not only dangerous, but not true.

> While some of what we know and can do is undoubtedly appropriate and timely for early adolescents, not all of it is.

The content presently "taught" in the curriculum reflects the interests, concerns, and values of adults, most often by deciding what they prize or like in their particular subject area. If we now introduce the questions and concerns of young people alongside those widely shared in the world and if we concentrate on content relevant to those, some currently "taught" content will surely not survive, especially that which has gotten on the agenda as we have increasingly played games of academic trivial pursuit in the interest of accommodating one or another mandate, interest group, or call for "rigor." Thus, part of our curriculum conversation must involve serious deliberation about what we think is really important by way of knowledge and skill and what might be judged inconsequential for young people in the middle school.

This last point is particularly important. As I continually think about the concept of integrated knowledge, I often find myself worrying about one or another piece of knowledge or skill that I like or think is important. Surely I am not alone in this. So it is especially critical that when this happens, we think about when that knowledge or skill became important to us, when we learned it, or when we came to like it. I suspect that quite often the answer is, "when we become adults." So we must continuously remind ourselves that early adolescents are not adults and that the middle school is not the end of schooling for most of them. While some of what we know and can do is undoubtedly appropriate and timely for early adolescents, not all of it is. To forget that would take us right back to the junior version of the high school and align us with those who seem to want to graduate school to start in the [sic] kindergarten.

However, in making decisions about curriculum content we must pay attention to an especially problematic situation. The knowledge and skills historically selected for inclusion in the curriculum as well as their organization into separate subjects, have been (and are) attached to the perceptions and values of those who are the gatekeepers of our society. I refer here to representatives of the dominant, high culture and those who have power in selecting and sorting people for privileged occupational positions. Both groups (and their membership overlaps to a great extent) have the largest measure of official control in naming what it is that young people need to have in order to gain access to a wide variety of places and positions in our society. For this reason, what they have to say cannot be underestimated or discounted.

Yet the concept of an integrative curriculum emerging from the real questions of young people and the larger world may not always naturally call forth some of the knowledge and skill prized by these gatekeepers. This poses a serious dilemma for those who have traditionally been denied access to privileged positions, that is those who are poor or of color and, of course, women. Even though we may legitimately question whether such people will have wide access to privilege anyway and whether such knowledge and skill is really needed by early adolescents, we are nevertheless compelled by present conditions in our society to see that it somehow has a place in the curriculum. To do otherwise would be to deny the perceptions of both privileged and non-privileged people and to leave the matter of access strictly up to the circumstance of who young people are born to and where they live.

Therefore, in the words of Leake (1991) and others, we must be careful that a different curriculum is not simply a case of "moving the target" just when some non-privileged people feel they have finally figured out what it might take for their children to have a chance. When I worked out the curriculum organization proposed a few years ago (Beane, 1990a), I suggested that the concerns of early adolescents were necessary, but not sufficient, for a significant curriculum, and thus included concerns from the larger world as another source. Among the latter was knowledge and skill from the dominant culture. In light of Leake's comment, I now want to reiterate strongly that I believe teachers, as professional educators and as participants in collaborative planning with young people, have not only a right, but an obligation to introduce some of that knowledge and skill. Otherwise we risk becoming another in a long line of liberal, "progressive" curriculum ideas that have backfired on some young people.

This obligation is a very serious one, although the tension it produces may be somewhat assuaged by remembering again that the middle school is not the only level of schooling and that the specialized curriculum of the high school offers a great deal along these lines. Nevertheless, our middle school curriculum conversation must take on questions about the knowledge and skill I am referring to here and how it might be brought into curriculum themes when it does not naturally arise.

The issues about content and skill that I have been outlining here may in one way be a bit less troublesome than we think. In the past few years, several national subject area associations have offered proposals that present new ways of thinking about various subjects. For example the National Council of Teachers of Mathematics has called for situating mathematics work in the context of communication, integration, exploration, and problem-solving. The National Council of Teachers of English has increasingly backed a broader view of language arts as well as a wholistic approach that attaches this area to others. The National Science Teachers Association has called for an end to the sequential, "layer-cake" approach to science and the repositioning of this area in terms of social issues, integration, and problem-solving. These are but a few examples of a trend toward seeing subject areas not as abstract and distinct, but as sources of knowledge and skill that might be used for larger purposes.

Interestingly, though, subject association spokespersons seem to have some difficulty imagining possible frameworks for integration that transcend subject areas. Perhaps it is the identities of the associations that keep them from doing so. One very obvious possibility, then, is to overcome the increasing trend of middle school people to talk only to each other and to invite the subject area associations to join our conversation in light of the integrative designs that are currently emerging within it.

SUBJECT AREAS AND TEACHER IDENTITIES

While the matter of what happens to content and skill is obviously a curriculum issue, it also involves the much understudied area of teacher self-concept and esteem. We should not underestimate the loyalty teachers have to the subject areas they have studied and taught nor the beliefs they hold about how important the content of particular areas are to the education of young people. Yet I think it is just as important to realize the extent to which subject areas enter into the identities of teachers; that is, so many identify themselves not simply as teachers but as teachers of particular subjects (e.g., "I am an art teacher, a mathematics teacher," and so on).

In everyday life of the school such subject-specific identities have even larger meaning in terms of the status differentiation among subjects: academics over "specials," mathematics and science as "most rigorous," physical education as "just games," or industrial arts as preparation for low-status work. And it is important to recognize that both the identities and status systems become tied to particular classrooms, scheduling priorities, grade weightings, grouping patterns, and other institutional gimmicks of the school. That such factors have helped to define the lives of teachers over their careers is clearly a part of the hidden curriculum in conversations about curriculum.

> Teachers who have seen themselves as subject specialists are asked literally to leave their teaching certificates at the classroom doors and enter instead as "teachers" in a generic sense.

Consider, then, some of the characteristics and conditions that have been attached to thinking about an integrative curriculum. Since knowledge and skill are not identified along subject area lines, teachers who have seen themselves as subject specialists are asked literally to leave their teaching certificates at the classroom doors and enter instead as "teachers" in a generic sense, whose work it is to help young people "search for self and social meaning." This implies that the knowledge and skill they will be involved with will be both broad and general, and without defined scope and sequence or even specified subject slots in the daily schedule. Add to this other concepts such as the teacher as facilitator, as learner, and so on, and the mood is enough to paralyze almost any workshop on curriculum reform.

While not discouraged by all of this, I am somewhat at a loss to suggest anything like a way out of it. Certainly there are some teachers who are more than happy to disregard their subject area identifications, having felt restricted by them anyway. Others may be willing to think about the possibility as a result of workshop experiences that demonstrate integrative curriculum approaches. Still others, probably more, might do so if they had the opportunity to use an integrative approach in collaboration with teachers who have previously done so. Aside from this we can surely depend only on the possibility that the stories of teachers who try this approach will encourage others to do so.

> In an integrated approach, the theme is named and clarified and then teachers proceed to identify the best possible activities they can think of for addressing it.

PLANNING FOR AN INTEGRATIVE CURRICULUM

Most so-called "interdisciplinary teams," when they do get around to the curriculum, begin their planning with a theme or topic and then ask what each subject area can contribute to the theme. While this sort of mild correlation is a dramatic step for some people, it still retains the place, space, and priority of the separate subjects. Furthermore, young people still experience school as a trip from one subject class to another where teachers more or less often remind them of their attachment to the theme at hand. For this reason, accurately naming this approach as "multi-disciplinary" or "multi-subject" is more than a semantic game.

In an integrated approach, the theme is named and clarified and then teachers proceed to identify the best possible activities they can think of for addressing it. They may at some point conduct an analysis to see what skills and knowledge are being used, but in bypassing the multi-disciplinary question, they begin to break down subject area lines. Young people experience this approach as movement from one activity to another, each related to the theme, rather than as a trip through a series of subject-identified classes.

In an integrative approach, where the questions and concerns of young people are taken seriously, the planning begins by asking them to say what those questions and concerns are and subsequently what themes they cluster around. Then the group, including teachers and young people, decides on activities they will use to address the themes and respond to the questions and concerns. The schedule is again organized around the activities rather than subject areas and the teachers may (and should) carry out some kind of knowledge/skill analysis in light of the issues I raised earlier.

Some teachers have decided to name themes and then ask young people to raise questions and concerns within or about it. Since there is no recipe for an integrative curriculum, I do not want to criticize this variation. However, I do think we have to be concerned about the need to be sure that such pre-planned themes have genuine personal and social significance and to leave open the later possibility of starting with the questions and concerns of young people as confidence is gained.

I mention this matter of planning here to remind us of the need to look to young people as a source for curriculum planning and also to say that we should be careful not to let people duck out of the curriculum conversation by way of mild correlations through multi-disciplinary thinking. If we really mean to be serious about this conversation, then that kind of backsliding will just not do.

CLASSROOM LIFE

Another issue I want to touch upon has to do with questions about whether the behavior of young people improves in classrooms where the integrative approach is used. Teachers who have tried this certainly do report a decline in, but not a disappearance of, disruptive incidents and referrals, and a belief that young people are more engaged. However, this may have to do with who these teachers are to begin with or that they no longer have time to deal with minor incidents. Or it may be that the curriculum really is at work here. Perhaps when such questions are raised, we would do well to remember that this is a theory of curriculum, not one of discipline or classroom management (although there is an implied relationship of adults and young people that is different from the adversarial one found in many classrooms).

Along those same lines, I also want to point out that those who see this approach as unstructured and careless could not be more wrong in their criticism. Asking young people to name questions and concerns they have about themselves and the world is not at all like asking something like, "What do you want to do today?" Nor as I have already pointed out, is the voice of the teacher omitted from the process. The point is that the integrative curriculum I am describing, and particularly the planning of it, is a quite tightly constructed way of creating the curriculum.

THE LARGER PURPOSE

In my small book, *A Middle School Curriculum: From Rhetoric to Reality* (Beane, 1990a), I mentioned that the concepts of democracy, human dignity, and cultural diversity ought to constantly come to life in whatever themes we finally work with. In bringing this paper to an end I want to return to that idea and thus remind us of a larger purpose in our work. As I have participated in classroom experiences with an integrative approach and read accounts of others, I am greatly encouraged by the possibilities this way of thinking has for the three concepts just mentioned.

First, the process associated with the integrative approach involves continuous collaborative planning with young people as well as an end to authoritarian rule by adults. Moreover, the approach emphasizes inquiry, cooperative problem-solving, and the personal and collective construction of meaning. Clearly, this kind of process brings to life the concept of authentic democratic principles while dignifying the place of young people in the school. I have been stunned to see not only the willingness of adults to abandon traditional power relations in their work with young people, but to avoid the subtle but equally authoritarian "engineering of consent" that has characterized much of so-called "cooperative planning" over the years. These teachers actually respect young people and, since they see themselves as members of the group, are not afraid that their own questions and concerns will be lost in the shuffle.

But more than that, I have been especially impressed by the kind of questions, concerns, and activities that have emerged in these classrooms. We have been right in trying to put an end to the "hormones with feet" and "brain dead" metaphors. These classrooms are full of content about justice, wealth, dignity, the environment, and prejudice of all kinds. I have seen young people, out of their own questions, develop concerns for non-privileged people, explore various cultures with respect, disdain injustice, debate free speech, become indignant at environmental destruction, demand an end to prejudice, and, in these and other ways, make their own classrooms a much prettier picture than the larger world in which we and they live.

> The kinds of questions and concerns our young people are raising demand that we make our whole agenda public.

I am concerned, though, that these possibilities are not explicit enough in our curriculum conversation. It is time we made them so, not only to clarify our own thinking, but for others to see how and why they may join us. This may seem to a be dangerous course of action since democracy, human dignity, and cultural diversity are so contentious these days. But imagine what it would mean if this larger part of our work were more explicit and those who oppose the work itself would thus have to stand against those themes. We may talk this issue through, but it is clear that the kinds of questions and concerns our young people are raising demand that we make our whole agenda public since these themes are clearly high on theirs.

IN CLOSING

I am well aware that while this paper has attempted to address many of the issues surrounding what is called an integrative curriculum, it has left more questions than it has answered. Yet this is exactly what is called for if our work is to involve a widely shared conversation about what ought to be the middle school curriculum. Moreover, this will continue to be the case if we take seriously the concept of parallel structure mentioned earlier. The fact is that the work to date offers no map to guide our thinking, only a compass. There are no recipes! But then, why should there be? The track record of highly specific, top-down curriculum proposals is miserable at best. Furthermore, such mandates are the major symbol of the disastrous trend to move curriculum decision making further and further from locations of young people and their teachers.

If we are to have any success in our efforts to clean up the middle school curriculum, we do need an overriding philosophy to guide us and the courage to say it publicly. But the matter of how that philosophy will be brought to life or just what the curriculum will look like in any one place must be worked out by the people in that place. So it is at this time that we must commit ourselves to conversations about the curriculum rather than simply looking for implementation solutions. And in doing so, we must somehow be willing to set aside the tendency to jam the concept of an integrative curriculum into the categories of our present subject-centered structures and even some of the innovative arrangements that have shown up in middle schools over the past few decades. If we really want the middle school curriculum our young people deserve, then it is time to let go and turn ourselves over to the more promising course of action that many middle level educators are beginning to take.

REFERENCES

Beane, J. A. (1990a). *A middle school curriculum: From rhetoric to reality.* Columbus, OH: National Middle School Association.

Beane, J. A. (1990b). *Affect in the curriculum: Toward democracy, dignity, and diversity.* New York: Teachers College Press.

Beane, J. A. (1991). The middle school: The natural home of integrated curriculum. *Education Leadership, 49,* 9-13.

Beane, J. A. (1992). Turning the floor over: Reflections on a middle school curriculum. *Middle School Journal, 23*(3), 34-40.

Brodhagen, B., Weilbacher, G., & Beane, J. (1992). Living in the future: An experiment with an integrative curriculum. *Dissemination Services on the Middle Grades, 23,* 1-7.

Dewey, J. (1938). *Experience and education.* New York: Macmillan.

Dressel, P. L. (1958). The meaning and significance of integration. In N. B. Henry (Ed.), *The integration of educational experiences,* 57th Yearbook of the National Society for the Study of Education. Chicago, IL: University of Chicago Press.

Hopkins, L. T. (1937). *Integration: Its meaning and application.* New York: Appleton-Century.

Leake, B. (1991). Speech to the National Middle School Association Regional Conference. Minneapolis, MN.

Stevenson, C., & Carr, J. (1993). *Integrative studies in the middle grades: Dancing through walls.* New York: Teachers College Press.

This paper was presented at the First Annual Curriculum Conversation, University of Wisconsin-Green Bay, January 1992.

Definitions in Perspective: Integration Is Not New

There are perhaps about one hundred billion neurons, or nerve cells, in the brain, and in a single human brain the number of possible interconnections between these cells is greater than the number of atoms in the universe.—Robert Ornstein & Richard Thompson, *The Amazing Brain*, 1984, p. 21

Integrated learning coincides with the very nature of the brain—the ability to make connections, see patterns, and make meaning of the world. In an attempt to define integrated curricula, quite an assortment of words are given in the literature. Among the synonyms for "integrated" commonly bantered about are: interwoven, holistic, connected, interdisciplinary, cross-disciplinary, multi-disciplinary, transdisciplinary, pluridisciplinary, shared, fused, and of course, thematic.

While the diversity of definition is somewhat disconcerting as one initially investigates the concept of integrated learning, that same diversity usually turns into a blessing in disguise. As one explores definitions and grapples with the idea of "exactly what do we mean by integrated curriculum," there is an opportunity to define it in ways that are relevant and meaningful to those about to use it.

It seems less important to have universal agreement on the term, "integrated curriculum" than it is to have all stakeholders reach some level of consensus about what they mean by the idea. In fact, without a shared understanding of "integrated learning," it will be quite an undertaking to achieve any significant implementation of the concept.

In a more lighthearted approach to a definition, the following analogy offers concrete visual images of the concept of integrated learning. One teacher team used the girdle to extrapolate the definitive elements: "Integrated curricula is like a girdle because both need to be connected; hold the whole together; and enhance the base."

Once the team sorts out the elements of the definition, it becomes a simple task to refine and use that definition in communication with others who will be involved, such as other staff, parents, community leaders, and the students themselves.

Remember, it's not the definition that is so critical, but the shared understanding of that definition; for the number of possible interconnections is limitless. Once teachers put their creativity to work, the integrated learning that results reflects the boundlessness of any creative endeavor.

To help illuminate the concept of integrated learning and to introduce some previously conceived definitions, Jacob's essay on integrated curriculum answers the question, "What is it?" The author implies that in its simplest form, integrated curriculum is making commonsense connections within the curricula.

Vars, on the other hand, places the integrated curriculum concept within the historical perspective of "all school themes, interdisciplinary teams, and block time," as part of the "core curriculum" approach. And, while Vars points out the historical precedence for integrated learning, Berlak and Berlak (in Shoemaker) present helpful comparisons of the principles and outcomes of integrative education as opposed to a traditional program. Within the analysis are eight issues, including control, content, motivation, and allocation of resources.

The Integrated Curriculum

by Heidi Hayes Jacobs

What it is, why your students need it.

Jody, a fourth grader, was emphatic. "Reading is not taught in science. That's different. Reading is stories, you know, fiction." David, her classmate, chimed in, "Reading is always after recess." I asked, "What is social studies then?" Renee said, "Social studies is when we work in groups, probably because it's social."

By third grade, children view subjects as changes in behavior, teacher attitude, areas of the room, and times of day. Rarely does anyone explain to them the nature and power of the disciplines or how the subjects relate to one another.

An interdisciplinary curriculum addresses this problem of fragmented schedules that shatter curriculum into isolated pieces of knowledge. Implementing interdisciplinary curriculum units helps children acquire targeted concepts and skills of various disciplines more effectively. Of course, there are times when skills and concepts are best addressed through the singular focus of one discipline. In essence then, both perspectives are necessary. This dual emphasis is different from past attempts at curriculum integration that viewed the two approaches as opposing points of view—through this century, there has been an unfortunate tendency for schools to go to extremes of either rigid subject isolation or strained, whimsical thematic instruction. Not any longer. Teachers across the country are carefully examining their curricula to provide students with both experiences.

From *Instructor* magazine, vol. 101, no. 2, p. 22-23, September 1991. Reprinted with permission.

Because curriculum is traditionally structured in discipline-specific formats, teachers implementing an interdisciplinary approach need to recognize possibilities for making connections within their curricula and plan units or courses to involve students in making connections among the disciplines.

The premise that underscores interdisciplinary programs is common sense, not ideology. (This is not a return to the open-classroom experiments of the '60s.) Both teachers and students need to make sensible connections among subjects. When a seventh grader studies a world-geography unit in October and a world-climate unit February, there is a conspicuous lack of common sense. However, a first grader reading Frank Asch's *Happy Birthday, Moon* (Simon and Schuster, 1982) as he or she studies the concept of "echoes" in a science unit on sound may approach the lessons with a sense of delight about the mystery of echoes. Deliberate planning that integrates two or more disciplines mutually reinforces concepts and skills.

> **Existing curriculum is the place to find interdisciplinary unit ideas—look for natural connections between required subject areas.**

DESIGNING INTERDISCIPLINARY UNITS

Existing curriculum is the place to find interdisciplinary unit ideas—look for natural connections between required subject areas. Current-events issues and student concerns are other subjects for units. Keep in mind that not all subject areas need to be included in a multidisciplinary unit. In fact, attempts to do so can yield some strained connections. For example, a second-grade unit on folklore has natural connections to literature, social studies, and the arts. But forcing an equal number of math activities may result in an artificial collection of activities rather than a carefully structured unit. The keys to effective unit design are:

- common planning time among participating teachers,
- flexible scheduling, and
- early assessment of the yearly curriculum.

This last point is especially important. By mapping out your curriculum choices on a monthly academic calendar you can more easily identify potential areas for interdisciplinary unit development based on what you are teaching (rather than attempting to insert something new in an already packed year).

Teachers involved in integrating curricula will find that rigor and imagination go hand-in-hand as they develop carefully crafted interdisciplinary units to help their students. And their students no doubt will appreciate the efforts. As a sixth grader, Rick, said, "You teachers should talk to each other. Sometimes you repeat things and sometimes things you teach could go together." Rick should be assured that we are talking to each other to make sense and to make connections in the curriculum. Integrating knowledge is basic to education.

Integrated Curriculum in Historical Perspective

by Gordon F. Vars

All-school themes, interdisciplinary teams, and block time are three alternative ways to effectively deliver a core curriculum, a concept with a long history.

Educators once more are seeking ways to help students make sense out of the multitude of life's experiences and the bits and pieces of knowledge being taught in the typical splintered, over-departmentalized school curriculum. To lessen some of the fragmentation, various types of integrative or holistic curriculums are being proposed, including the distinct form of "core curriculum," which focuses directly on the problems, issues, and concerns of students.

Organizing a school staff to deliver a core curriculum takes essentially three different forms (Vars 1969, 1986, 1987). In the total staff approach, all or most of the school's staff agrees to deal with some aspect of an all-school theme or topic for a brief period of time. For example, in the Martin Luther King Laboratory School of Evanston, Illinois, students in grades K-8 spent several weeks during one year studying life in the United States during the Roaring Twenties. Each year, the staff may select a new theme.

In the interdisciplinary team approach, teachers of several different subjects are assigned one group of students and encouraged to correlate at least some of their teaching. At Horizon High School in Brighton, Colorado, teachers of 10th grade English, social studies, and science organize instruction around a series of themes, such as Change, Interdependence, or Patterns.

From *Educational Leadership*, vol. 49, no. 2, p. 14-15, 1991.
Reprinted with permission.

The third option makes use of block-time and self-contained classes, giving one teacher responsibility for instruction in several subjects during an extended segment of time. For example, teachers of 7th and 8th grade Common Learnings at South Junior High School in Lawrence, Kansas, teach students both language arts and social studies during a two-hour block of time. The degree to which the two subjects are integrated varies from teacher to teacher.

DESIGNS FOR AN INTEGRATIVE CURRICULUM

Each of these staffing arrangements can be used with a variety of integrative curriculum designs (Vars 1987). In the simplest approach—correlation—teachers of different subjects all deal with aspects of one topic at the same time, like the Roaring Twenties theme mentioned earlier. Fusion takes integration a step further by combining the content of two or more subjects into a new course with a new name, such as Common Learnings or American Studies.

> In core, the curriculum design begins with the students and the society in which they live.

The concept of core curriculum is a full and important step beyond either correlation or fusion. In core, the curriculum design begins with the students and the society in which they live. Needs, problems, and concerns of a particular group of students are identified, and skills and subject matter from any pertinent subject are brought in to help students deal with those matters. Staff members may identify a cluster of student concerns or needs that are typical of the age group and design units of study that promise to be relevant to students. Even in this "structured core" approach, however, teachers adapt the unit to the particular students they have in each class.

The ultimate in student-centered integrative curriculum is "unstructured core," in which teacher and students together develop units of study. The only restrictions are that the study must be worthwhile, doable, and appropriate for the students' level of maturity. The basic technique for developing one of these units or for adapting a pre-planned unit to a particular class is teacher-student planning (Parrish and Waskin 1967). The teacher and students jointly decide on specific questions for study, how the unit will be carried out, and how student progress will be evaluated.

THE EVOLVING CONCEPT OF CORE

Efforts to integrate the curriculum have a long history. Stack (1961) traced the philosophical and psychological antecedents of the core curriculum as far back as the writing of Herbert Spencer in the 1800s. Harville (1954) cited early 20th century trends in education, psychology, and anthropology. Fraley (1978) described the work of Hollis Caswell and Harold Alberty on behalf of an integrated core curriculum. In their major work on core curriculum, Faunce and Bossing (1958) described a variety of state and national curriculum reform efforts of the 1930s and 1940s. The most important of these, the progressive education movement, included a strong emphasis on student-centered, integrative approaches to education, usually under the name of core curriculum (Vars 1972).

The evolving concept of core curriculum was tested in the famous Eight-Year Study of the Progressive Education Association (Aiken 1942). Since then, more than 80 normative or comparative studies have been carried out on the effectiveness of integrative programs (National Association for Core Curriculum 1984). In nearly every instance, students in various types of integrative/interdisciplinary programs have performed as well or better on standardized achievement tests than students enrolled in the usual separate subjects.

THE CONTINUING CHALLENGE

Despite solid research support, the popularity of core-type integrative programs waxes and wanes from year to year, as education shifts primary attention from student concerns to subject matter acquisition to social problems and back again. The continuing challenge is to design curriculums that simultaneously take into account solid subject matter, the needs of the learner, and society's problems.

REFERENCES

Aiken, W. (1942). *The Story of the Eight-Year Study.* New York: Harper.

Faunce, R.C., and N. L. Bossing. (1958). *Developing the Core Curriculum.* 2nd ed. Englewood Cliffs, N.J.: Prentice-Hall.

Fraley, A. E. (1978). "Core Curriculum: An Epic in the History of Educational Reform." Doctoral diss., Teachers College, Columbia University. *Dissertation Abstracts International* 38, 10: 5883A. (University Microfilms No. 78-04457).

Harville, H. (1954). "Origins of the Core Concept." *Social Education* 18, 4: 161-163.

National Association for Core Curriculum. (1984). *Bibliography of Research on the Effectiveness of Block-Time, Core, and Interdisciplinary Team Teaching Programs.* Kent, Ohio: NACC.

Parrish, L., and Y. Waskin. (1967). *Teacher-Pupil Planning for Better Classroom Learning.* New York: Pitman.

Stack, E.C. (1961). "The Philosophical and Psychological Antecedents of the Core Curriculum in Educational Theory, 1800-1918." Doctoral diss., University of North Carolina. *Dissertation Abstracts International* 20: 1830-1831. (University Microfilms No. 60-4869).

Vars, G.F., ed. (1969). *Common Learnings: Core and Interdisciplinary Team Approaches.* Scranton, Pa.: Intext.

Vars, G.F. (1972). "Curriculum in Secondary Schools and Colleges." In *A New Look at Progressive Education,* 1972 ASCD Yearbook, edited by James R. Squire. Alexandria, Va.: Association for Supervision and Curriculum Development.

Vars, G.F., ed. (1986). "Integrating the Middle Grades Curriculum." *Transescence* 14, 1: 3-31.

Vars, G.F. (1987). *Interdisciplinary Teaching in the Middle Grades: Why and How.* Columbus, Ohio: National Middle School Association.

Author's note: This article is expcerpted from "Current Concepts of Core Curriculum: Alternative Designs for Integrative Programs," a special issue of *Transescence* (in press). Used with permission.

A Comparison of Traditional and Integrative Approaches

by Betty Jean Eklund Shoemaker

To further understand integrative education, it is helpful to compare and contrast its principles and outcomes with those of current (traditional) programs. Berlak and Berlak (1981) have identified several philosophical, psychological, and social assumptions on which practical issues in schools are based. They identify a total of sixteen issues, of which I have adapted eight to serve as dimensions for comparing traditional and integrative approaches.

CHILD AS STUDENT VS. WHOLE CHILD

In traditional education, the child is seen not as a whole person but only in her or his role as a student; current programs generally are discipline-based and emphasize intellectual development. The emphasis of integrative models is to educate the whole child. Intellectual development cannot be isolated from emotional, social, physical, and moral development.

TEACHER CONTROL VS. SHARED CONTROL

The teacher retains control of both learning and behavioral standards in traditional programs. She or he generally plays a strong directive role in delivering instruction. In integrative models the student, the parents, and the teacher share control and responsibility for the learning environment. Students are encouraged to experiment and try out various strategies and work cooperatively.

From *Integrative Education: A Curriculum for the Twenty-First Century*, Betty Jean Eklund Shoemaker, October 1989, p. 39-41. Reprinted with permission.

PUBLIC VS. PERSONAL AND PUBLIC KNOWLEDGE

Little room is allowed for pursuit of personal interests within traditional subject-based disciplines. Within integrative programs there is an emphasis on both personal and public knowledge. Student-initiated interests and projects are seen as vehicles for teaching valid contents within the public arena.

KNOWLEDGE AS CONTENT VS. KNOWLEDGE AS PROCESS

Within many current programs, knowledge is seen as mastery of a prescribed, fixed set of content organized into subjects and textbooks. With the amount of knowledge doubling every fifteen to eighteen months, the curriculum has become overcrowded. Debate centers around what content knowledge should be taught and what content knowledge should be eliminated. Within integrative programs, knowledge is seen as an understanding of the connectedness of "big ideas" and "concepts." Students are encouraged to use a variety of strategies in problem-solving. The process of arriving at solutions is as important as the product.

> Within integrative programs, knowledge is seen as an understanding of the connectedness of "big ideas" and "concepts."

EXTRINSIC VS. INTRINSIC MOTIVATION

Many current programs rely heavily on extrinsic rewards such as grades and reinforcers. Integrative programs actively involve the learner and focus on student interests and concerns that lead to intrinsic motivation.

MOLECULAR VS. HOLISTIC TEACHING AND LEARNING

Learning is broken down into small elements and taught sequentially in traditional programs. Students are viewed as competent when they have mastered the individual pieces of the curriculum. This has led to fragmentation both within the curriculum and the school day. Most integrative programs emphasize holistic teaching and learning, using a variety of teaching strategies and thematic approaches. Instructional blocks are longer and there is less movement from class to class. Learning is seen as occurring in a context where students are able to relate new material to already-existing knowledge. A molecular approach is used occasionally in integrative settings, but instruction consistently moves toward a holistic view.

SHARED VS. UNIQUE CHARACTERISTICS OF CHILDREN
Current educational programs see students as having many shared characteristics. This is evidenced by the heavy reliance on textbooks where all students are expected to master the same material. Within integrative models children are viewed as having both shared characteristics developmentally and having unique characteristics reflected in particular learning styles. Heterogeneous grouping is valued.

DIFFERENTIAL VS. EQUAL ALLOCATION OF RESOURCES
Both teacher and school resources tend to be allocated unequally in current educational programs. Tracking students within particular ability groups provides learners with different types of teacher attention and access to different skills and knowledge. Organizing knowledge into linear academic disciplines has led to the development of certain authority structures in which certain types of knowledge are accorded greater respect and value than others. Sciences are valued higher than the humanities in secondary schools, and reading and mathematics outrank the arts at the primary level. Corresponding differences in the relative positions of power of teaching positions can also be observed. Moreover, there is great competition between subject areas over the allocation of school resources—both in time and materials. Pie charts with time allocation percentages listed are common.

Integrative models tend to reflect a common curriculum in which tracking and departmentalization are avoided. Generalists and specialists are seen as members of one team collaborating to effectively plan and deliver instruction. (Refer to the work of Basil Bernstein [1971] in *Knowledge and Control* edited by Michael Young, for a more detailed discussion of this significant point.)

In summary, current programs and practices are content driven, are fragmented, reflect centralized control, track children, and involve competition to gain access to resources. Integrative programs and practices are theme-based, are holistic, reflect shared control, and nurture all children in collaborative, interactive environments.

Models for Planning:
It's Just Common Sense

Upon this gifted age, in its dark hour,
Falls from the sky a meteoric shower
Of facts...they lie unquestioned, uncombined
Wisdom enough to leech us of our ill
Is daily spun; but there exists no loom
To weave it into fabric...—Edna St. Vincent Millay

To take the disparate pieces of information, the data and facts that bombard the student from every discipline, and to make sense of all that within the mind is at once the mission of the teacher and the goal of the students

Both have critical roles. The teacher is the architect of the intellect, designing curriculum and instruction that invite the learner to make connections. In this scenario, the teacher designs learning with deliberate attention to external, overt connections within and across subject-matter content. In turn, the student becomes the capable apprentice. The student receives the external data and continues the connection-making inside his own mind—trying to link new information with prior knowledge and then apply the emerging ideas to novel situations.

In order to make external connections throughout the teaching day, teachers are looking for simple structure and viable models to help them manipulate their subject matter. This manipulation of content functions like a kaleidoscope. The fragments of curriculum remain constant, similar to the chips of glass in the kaleidoscope. Each shift of the cylinder reveals a stunning new design just as each shift in curriculum planning reveals a stunning new arrangement of that content. Just as the images in the kaleidoscope retain their separate pieces and yet are enhanced by the changes, so too does the curricula become enhanced. Nothing is lost in integrated learning...learning is only enriched and enhanced.

Providing a spectrum of models for teachers to use in planning for integrated learning is the essay, "Ten Ways to Integrate the Curricula." In this concise piece, Fogarty develops ten views for integrating the curricula and poses the question "How do you see it?" Included among the ten models are the connected, nested, webbed, threaded, and immersed. All models are defined and illustrated with graphic organizers for immediate teacher use.

In a second essay, Shoemaker presents an introduction to eight models that are concept-based interpretations of designs for integrated learning. Among the eight terms are infusion, thematic, holistic, and integrative brainwork. The piece ends with a look at a planning guide of major themes and concepts, organized by curriculum.

Both articles in this section provide the reader with practical, hands-on ideas for beginning to integrate the curricula. However, both authors imply that there are as many ways to design curricula as there are creative teachers.

Tens Ways to Integrate Curriculum

by Robin Fogarty

These 10 models give school faculties a solid foundation for designing curriculums that help their students make valuable connections while learning.

> To the young mind everything is individual, stands by itself. By and by, it finds how to join two things and see in them one nature; then three, then three thousand...discovering roots running underground whereby contrary and remote things cohere and flower out from one stem.... The astronomer discovers that geometry, a pure abstraction of the human mind, is the measure of planetary motion. The chemist finds proportions and intelligible method throughout matter; and science is nothing but the finding of analogy, identity, in the most remote parts.— Emerson

To help the young mind discover "roots running underground whereby contrary and remote things cohere and flower out from one stem" is the mission of both teachers and learners. Educators can achieve this mission, in part, by integrating the curriculum. The 10 models described here present ways along a continuum to accomplish this (Figure 1).

Beginning with an exploration *within single disciplines* (the fragmented, connected, and nested models), and continuing with models that integrate *across several disciplines* (the sequenced, shared, webbed, threaded, and integrated models), the continuum ends with models that operate *within* learners themselves (the immersed model) and finally *across* networks of learners (the networked model). Figure 2 briefly describes and

From *Educational Leadership*, vol. 49, no. 2, p. 61-65, 1991.
Reprinted with permission.

Figure 1

How to Integrate the Curriculum

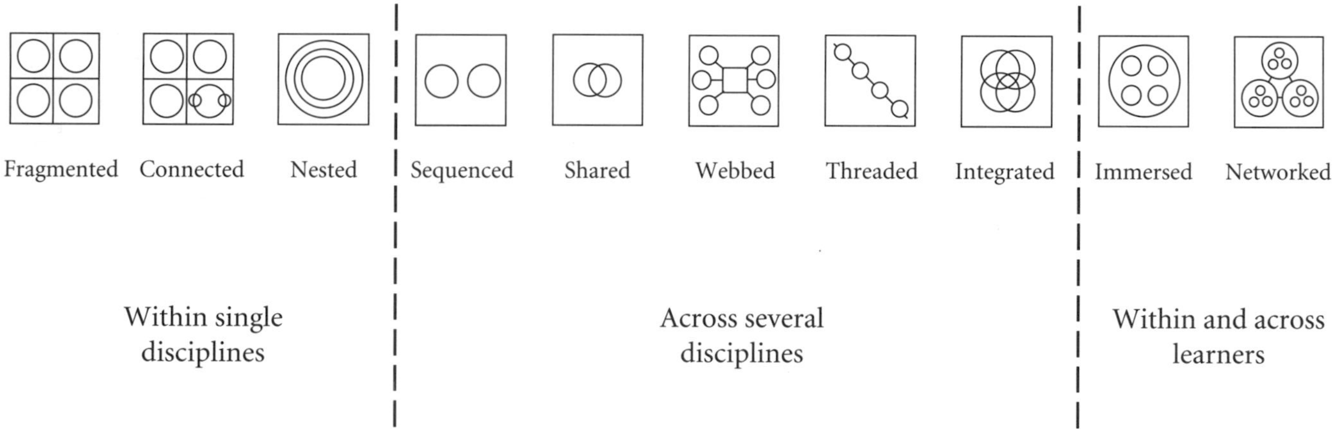

Fragmented   Connected   Nested   Sequenced   Shared   Webbed   Threaded   Integrated   Immersed   Networked

Within single disciplines

Across several disciplines

Within and across learners

Reprinted with permission from: *The Mindful School: How to Integrate the Curricula* by Robin Fogarty, (Palatine, Ill.: Skylight Publishing, Inc., 1991), p. xiv.

Toward an Integrated Curriculum
Ten Views for Integrating the Curriculum: How Do You See It?

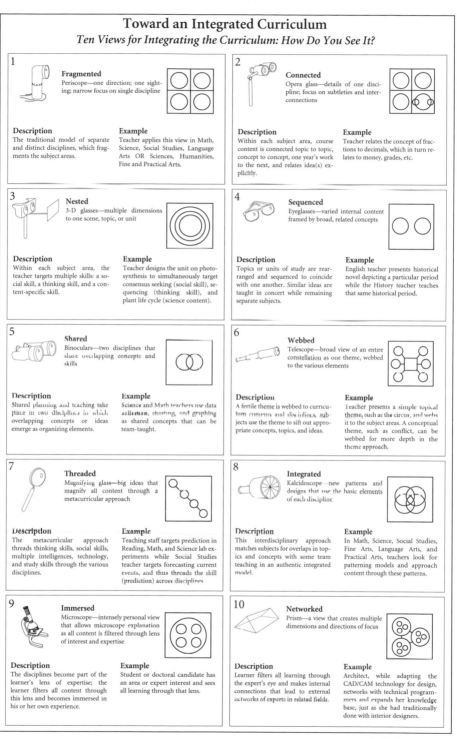

1 Fragmented
Periscope—one direction; one sighting; narrow focus on single discipline

Description
The traditional model of separate and distinct disciplines, which fragments the subject areas.

Example
Teacher applies this view in Math, Science, Social Studies, Language Arts OR Sciences, Humanities, Fine and Practical Arts.

2 Connected
Opera glass—details of one discipline; focus on subtleties and interconnections

Description
Within each subject area, course content is connected topic to topic, concept to concept, one year's work to the next, and relates idea(s) explicitly.

Example
Teacher relates the concept of fractions to decimals, which in turn relates to money, grades, etc.

3 Nested
3-D glasses—multiple dimensions to one scene, topic, or unit

Description
Within each subject area, the teacher targets multiple skills: a social skill, a thinking skill, and a content-specific skill.

Example
Teacher designs the unit on photosynthesis to simultaneously target consensus seeking (social skill), sequencing (thinking skill), and plant life cycle (science content).

4 Sequenced
Eyeglasses—varied internal content framed by broad, related concepts

Description
Topics or units of study are rearranged and sequenced to coincide with one another. Similar ideas are taught in concert while remaining separate subjects.

Example
English teacher presents historical novel depicting a particular period while the History teacher teaches that same historical period.

5 Shared
Binoculars—two disciplines that share overlapping concepts and skills

Description
Shared planning and teaching take place in two disciplines in which overlapping concepts or ideas emerge as organizing elements.

Example
Science and Math teachers use data collection, charting, and graphing as shared concepts that can be team-taught.

6 Webbed
Telescope—broad view of an entire constellation as one theme, webbed to the various elements

Description
A fertile theme is webbed to curriculum contents and disciplines; subjects use the theme to sift out appropriate concepts, topics, and ideas.

Example
Teacher presents a simple topical theme, such as the circus, and webs it to the subject areas. A conceptual theme, such as conflict, can be webbed for more depth in the theme approach.

7 Threaded
Magnifying glass—big ideas that magnify all content through a metacurricular approach

Description
The metacurricular approach threads thinking skills, social skills, multiple intelligences, technology, and study skills through the various disciplines.

Example
Teaching staff targets prediction in Reading, Math, and Science lab experiments while Social Studies teacher targets forecasting current events, and thus threads the skill (prediction) across disciplines

8 Integrated
Kaleidoscope—new patterns and designs that use the basic elements of each discipline

Description
This interdisciplinary approach matches subjects for overlaps in topics and concepts with some team teaching in an authentic integrated model.

Example
In Math, Science, Social Studies, Fine Arts, Language Arts, and Practical Arts, teachers look for patterning models and approach content through these patterns.

9 Immersed
Microscope—intensely personal view that allows microscope explanation as all content is filtered through lens of interest and expertise

Description
The disciplines become part of the learner's lens of expertise; the learner filters all content through this lens and becomes immersed in his or her own experience.

Example
Student or doctoral candidate has an area or expert interest and sees all learning through that lens.

10 Networked
Prism—a view that creates multiple dimensions and directions of focus

Description
Learner filters all learning through the expert's eye and makes internal connections that lead to external networks of experts in related fields.

Example
Architect, while adapting the CAD/CAM technology for design, networks with technical programmers and expands her knowledge base, just as she had traditionally done with interior designers.

© Robin Fogarty, 1991*

*Extrapolated from "Design Options for an Integrated Curriculum" by Heidi Hayes Jacobs in *Interdisciplinary Curriculum*, Alexandria, VA: ASCD, 1989. Reprinted with permission from: *The Mindful School: How to Integrate the Curricula* by Robin Fogarty, (Palatine, Ill.: Skylight Publishing, Inc., 1991), p. *xv*.

provides an example of each of the 10 models that teachers can use to design integrated curriculums.

THE FRAGMENTED MODEL

The *fragmented* model, the traditional design for organizing the curriculum, dictates separate and distinct disciplines. This model views the curriculum through a periscope, offering one sighting at a time: one directed focus on a single discipline. Typically, the major academic areas are math, science, language arts, and social studies. Each is seen as a pure entity in and of itself. Relationships between subject areas—physics and chemistry, for example—are only implicitly indicated.

In middle and secondary schools, the disciplines are taught by different teachers in different locations, with students moving from room to room. Each separate encounter has a distinct cellular organization, leaving students with a fragmented view of the curriculum. A less severe model of fragmentation prevails in elementary classrooms, where the teacher says, "Now, put away your math books, and take out your science packets." The daily schedule shows a distinct time slot for each subject, with topics from two areas only occasionally related intentionally.

A high school student explained the fragmented curriculum like this: "Math isn't science, science isn't English, English isn't history. A subject is something you take once and need never take again. It's like getting a vaccination; I've had my shot of algebra. I'm done with that."

Despite the drawbacks of this traditional model, teachers can use it, individually or with colleagues, by listing and ranking curricular topics, concepts, or skills. In this way, teachers or teacher teams can begin to sift out curricular priorities within their own content areas—a much-needed first step.

THE CONNECTED MODEL

The *connected* model of the integrated curriculum is the view through an opera glass, providing a close-up of the details, subtleties, and interconnections within one discipline. While the disciplines remain separate, this model focuses on making explicit connections within each subject area—connecting one topic, one skill, one concept to the next; connecting one day's work, or even one semester's ideas, to the next. The key to this model is the deliberate effort to relate ideas within the discipline, rather than assuming that students will automatically understand the connections.

In middle or secondary school, for example, the earth science teacher could relate the geology unit to the astronomy unit by emphasizing the evolutionary nature of each. This similarity between the two units then becomes an organizer for students as they work through both. Teachers help students make connections by explicitly making links between subject areas.

THE NESTED MODEL

The *nested* model of integration views the curriculum through three-dimensional glasses, targeting multiple dimensions of a lesson. Nested integration takes advantage of natural combinations. For example, an elementary lesson on the circulatory system could target the concept of systems, as well as facts and understandings about the circulatory system in particular. In addition to this conceptual target, teachers can target the thinking skill cause and effect as well.

> The *nested* model of integration views the curriculum through three-dimensional glasses, targeting multiple dimensions of a lesson. Nested integration takes advantage of natural combinations.

Another example might be a lesson in a high school computer science class that targets the CAD/CAM (computer-assisted design/computer-assisted manufacturing) programs. As the students learn the workings of the program, the teacher can target the thinking skill of "envisioning" for explicit exploration and practice. In this nested approach, students in the computer class may also by instructed in ergonomics as they design furniture for schools of the future.

THE SEQUENCED MODEL

The *sequenced* model views the curriculum through eyeglasses: the lenses are separate but connected by a common frame. Although topics or units are taught separately, they are rearranged and sequenced to provide a broad framework for related concepts. Teachers can arrange topics so that similar units coincide. In the self-contained classroom, for example, *Charlotte's Web* can accompany the unit on spiders. *Johnny Tremain* can parallel the study of the Revolutionary War. The graphing unit can coincide with data collection in the weather unit. In secondary school, one might synchronize study of the stock market in math class with study of the Depression in history.

John Adams once said, "The textbook is not a moral contract that teachers are obliged to teach—teachers are obliged to teach children." Following the sequence of the textbook may work well in some cases, but it might make more sense to rearrange the sequence of units in other cases. The new sequence may be more logical if it parallels the presentation of other content *across* disciplines.

THE SHARED MODEL

The *shared* model views the curriculum through binoculars, bringing two distinct disciplines together into a single focused image. Using overlapping concepts as organizing elements, this model involves shared planning or teaching in two disciplines.

In middle and secondary schools, cross-departmental partners might plan a unit of study. The two members of the team approach the preliminary planning session with a notion of key concepts, skills, and attitudes traditionally taught in their single-subject approach. As the pair identify priorities, they look for overlaps in content. For example, the literature teacher might select the concept of The American Dream as an organizer for a collection of short stories by American authors. At the same time, the history teacher might note that his unit on American history could also use The American Dream as a unifying theme. In this way, the literature teacher and the history teacher team up to point out commonalities to students.

Elementary models of shared curriculums may embody standard planning models already in wide use. Typically, whole-language curriculums draw upon many curricular areas. The self-contained classroom teacher might plan a science unit (simple machines) and a social studies unit (the industrial revolution) around the concept of efficiency models. Teachers may ask themselves and each other: "What concepts do these units share?" "Are we teaching similar skills?"

THE WEBBED MODEL

The *webbed* model of integration views the curriculum through a telescope, capturing an entire constellation of disciplines at once. Webbed curriculums usually use a fertile theme to inte-

Figure 3

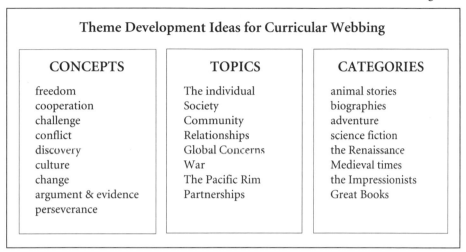

Theme Development Ideas for Curricular Webbing

CONCEPTS	TOPICS	CATEGORIES
freedom	The individual	animal stories
cooperation	Society	biographies
challenge	Community	adventure
conflict	Relationships	science fiction
discovery	Global Concerns	the Renaissance
culture	War	Medieval times
change	The Pacific Rim	the Impressionists
argument & evidence	Partnerships	Great Books
perseverance		

Reprinted with permission from: *The Mindful School: How to Integrate the Curricula* by Robin Fogarty, (Palatine, Ill.: Skylight Publishing, Inc., 1991), p. 55.

grate subject matter, such as Inventions. Once a cross-departmental team has chosen a theme, the members use it as an overlay to the different subjects. Inventions, for example, leads to the study of simple machines in science, to reading and writing about inventors in language arts, to designing and building models in industrial arts, to drawing and studying Rube Goldberg contraptions in math, and to making flowcharts in computer technology class.

In departmentalized situations, the webbed curricular approach to integration is often achieved through the use of a generic but fertile theme such as Patterns. The conceptual theme provides rich possibilities for the various disciplines.

While similar conceptual themes such as Patterns provide fertile ground for cross-disciplinary units of study, one can also use a book or a genre of books as the topic, to organize the curriculum thematically. For example, fairy tales or dog stories can become catalysts for curricular webbing. Figure 3 shows typical lists for theme development.

THE THREADED MODEL
The *threaded* model of integration views the curriculum through a magnifying glass: the "big ideas" are enlarged throughout all content with a metacurricular approach. This model threads thinking skills, social skills, study skills, graphic

organizers, technology, and a multiple intelligences approach to learning throughout all disciplines. The threaded model supersedes all subject matter content. For example, "prediction" is a skill used to estimate in mathematics, forecast in current events, anticipate in a novel, and hypothesize in the science lab. Consensus-seeking strategies are used in resolving conflicts in any problem-solving situation.

Using the idea of a metacurriculum, grade-level or interdepartmental teams can target a set of thinking skills to infuse into existing content priorities. For example, using a thinking skills curriculum, the freshman team might choose to infuse the skill of analysis into each content area.

As thinking skills or social skills are threaded into the content, teachers ask students: "How did you think about that?" "What thinking skill did you find most helpful?" "How well did your group work today?" These processing questions contrast sharply with the usual cognitive questions such as, "What answer did you get?

THE INTEGRATED MODEL

The *integrated* model views the curriculum through a kaleidoscope: interdisciplinary topics are rearranged around overlapping concepts and emergent patterns and designs. Using a cross-disciplinary approach, this model blends the four major disciplines by finding the overlapping skills, concepts, and attitudes in all four. As in the shared model, the integration is a result of sifting related ideas out of subject matter content. The integration sprouts from within the various disciplines, and teachers make matches among them as commonalties emerge.

> Interdisciplinary topics are rearranged around overlapping concepts and emergent patterns and designs.

At the middle or secondary school, an interdisciplinary team discovers they can apply the concept of argument and evidence in math, science, language arts, and social studies. In the elementary classroom, an integrated model that illustrates the critical elements of this approach is the whole language strategy, in which reading, writing, listening, and speaking skills spring from a holistic, literature-based program.

THE IMMERSED MODEL

The *immersed* model of integration views the curriculum through a microscope. In an intensely personal way, it filters all content through the lens of interest and expertise. In this model, integration takes place *within* learners, with little or no outside intervention.

Aficionados, graduate students, doctoral candidates, and post-doctoral fellows are totally immersed in a field of study. They integrate all data by funneling them through this area of intense interest. For example, a doctoral candidate may be a specialist in the chemical bonding of substances. Even though her field is chemistry, she devours the software programs in computer science classes so she can simulate lab experiments, saving days of tedious lab work. She learns patent law in order to protect the ideas for her company and to avoid liability cases.

Likewise, a 6-year-old writes incessantly about butterflies, spiders, insects, and creepy-crawlies of all sorts. Her artwork is modeled on the symmetrical design of ladybugs and the patterns of butterflies. She counts, mounts, and frames bugs; she even sings about them. Her interest in insect biology is already consuming her. The books she chooses reflect her internal integration of information around her pet subject.

An immersed learner might say, "It is a labor of love. It seems that everything I *choose* to pursue with any fervor is directly related to my field." Just as writers record notes and artists make sketches, immersed learners are constantly making connections to their subjects.

THE NETWORKED MODEL

The *networked* model of integration views the curriculum through a prism, creating multiple dimensions and directions of focus. Like a three- or four-way conference call, it provides various avenues of exploration and explanation. In this model, learners direct the integration process. Only the learners themselves, knowing the intricacies and dimensions of their field, can target the necessary resources, as they reach out within and across their areas of specialization.

The networked model is seen to a limited extent in elementary schools. Imagine a 5th grader who has had a keen interest in Native Americans since his toddler days of playing cowboys and Indians. His passion for Indian lore leads him into histori-cal readings—both fictional and nonfictional. Aware of his in-terest, his family hears about an archeological dig that recruits youngsters as part of a summer program. As a result of this summer "camp," this learner meets people in a number of fields: an anthropologist, a geologist, an archeologist, and an il-lustrator. Already this learner's networks are taking shape.

USING THE MODELS

Whether you are working alone, with partners, or in teams, the 10 organizers presented here can function as useful prototypes. In fact, a faculty can easily work with them over time to develop an integrated curriculum throughout the school. Each staff member or team might choose one model to work with each se-mester. As teachers begin the conversation about integrating the curriculum, they can work with the models to explore the con-nections within and across disciplines and within and across learners.

These models are just beginnings. Teachers should go on to invent their own designs for integrating the curriculum. The process itself never ends. It's a cycle that offers renewed energy to each school year as teachers help the young mind discover "roots running underground whereby contrary and remote things cohere and flower out from one stem."

Author's note: This article was adapted from the book *The Mindful School: How to Integrate the Curricula* (Palatine, IL: IRI/Skylight Publishing, Inc.).

Education 2000 Integrated Curriculum

by Betty Jean Eklund Shoemaker

Jessica Hall, a fifth-grader at Willagillespie Elementary School in Eugene, Oregon, recently wrote in her journal: "I have learned a lot since the last trimester. The whole school has been learning about 'form.' We learned about patterns in art, movement, and nature, and we just started learning about our body clocks. It's kind of nice to have one main thing to learn about. That way, it seems a lot easier to remember all that we've been taught."

Jessica's attitude is shared by many of her classmates and teachers as well as by a growing number of educators across America. Interest in the integrated curriculum is growing at all levels of schooling. In recent years, a number of national curriculum reports have called for an "integrated day," an "integrated curriculum," and the "integration" of a variety of materials or strategies into the school program.[1] Many districts, determined to prepare students more adequately for the 21st century, are restructuring their curricula to reflect this interest.[2]

In 1985 Margaret Nichols, the superintendent of the Eugene Public Schools, commissioned an extensive three-year study of elementary programs, which culminated in the publication of the report *Education 2000: Designing Our Future*.[3] One of the first recommendations of the

> Interest in the integrated curriculum is growing at all levels of schooling...Many districts, determined to prepare students more adequately for the 21st century, are restructuring their curricula to reflect this interest.

From *Phi Delta Kappan*, vol. 72, no. 10, p. 793-797, June 1991.
Reprinted with permission.

report was to replace the district's detailed, fragmented, specific curriculum with a concepts-based, integrated, general curriculum.

Since the publication of the report, I have worked with Eugene educators to develop and implement an integrated curriculum. In this article, I will clarify the various interpretations of *integration*, briefly review related research, and describe the curriculum that has been adopted by the Eugene Public Schools.

THE TERMINOLOGY

In our work to develop a concepts-based, integrated curriculum, it became increasingly obvious that, although integrative education was gaining national popularity, there were many different views of what it entailed and an equal number of terms to describe the various ways it might be approached. Our first task was to identify and define the different approaches.

• *Infusion* approaches integrate a particular subject (such as writing or thinking skills) across the curriculum.

• *Topics-within-disciplines* approaches integrate multiple strands of the same discipline within the instructional setting. Examples include integrated language arts and integrated mathematics programs.

• *Interdisciplinary* approaches maintain traditional subject boundaries while aligning content and concepts from one discipline with those of another.

• *Thematic* approaches subordinate subject matter to a theme, allowing the boundaries between disciplines to blur. Topics can be narrowly or broadly focused.

• *Holistic* approaches represent two perspectives: addressing the needs of the whole child (the integration of cognitive, physical, affective, moral, and spiritual dimensions) and offering a curriculum that provides the context in which new knowledge makes sense.

• *The mind/brain function* approach uses instructional strategies and classroom organization that engage students in using the four mind/brain functions identified by Barbara Clark.

• *Integrative brainwork* approaches use such information processing strategies as concept attainment, inductive thinking, advance organizers, concept mapping, and clinical interviews.

• *Combined* approaches incorporate aspects of several of the approaches mentioned above. Eugene's Education 2000 Integrated Curriculum is a good example of a combined approach.

BRAIN RESEARCH AND LEARNING

In developing the Education 2000 Integrated Curriculum, we reviewed the research on the human brain. Renate Caine and Geoffrey Caine synthesized the following principles, which have implications for applying learning theory in the classroom.[4]

Learning is a physiological experience that involves the entire organism. Anything that affects our physiology or our emotional state also affects our capacity to learn. Thus schools must take into account all facets of students' health and well-being and acknowledge differences in maturation among children. Teachers must also create learning environments characterized by support and mutual respect.

The search for meaning is basic to the human brain. The brain attends to the familiar at the same time that it seeks out the novel and the challenging. In addition, the brain finds meaning by discerning and creating patterns; it resists learning meaningless, isolated pieces of information. Thus schools should provide a combination of familiar, well-understood material and complex, meaningful challenges.

The brain has memory systems for processing rote learning and for instant recall or spatial memory. Facts and skills that are presented in isolation need more practice and rehearsal to be stored in the brain than does information presented in a meaningful context. Learning that takes place through actual experience and that draws on previous knowledge allows us to use our spatial memory, which is a very efficient use of the brain. This means that the brain understands and remembers best when learning is embedded in spatial memory. Thus teachers should increase the use of "real-life" experiences in the classroom.

The brain performs many functions simultaneously. Good teaching should orchestrate this parallel processing by using diverse methods and approaches. The brain also processes parts and wholes simultaneously. Good teaching neglects neither parts nor wholes and leads to learning that is cumulative and developmental. The brain not only absorbs information directly presented, but it also attends to information beyond the immediate focus of attention. The teacher should organize the learning environment to accommodate stimuli outside of the learner's direct attention. The brain responds well to challenges but is less effective when threatened. The teacher should reduce the conditions that create perceived threat and should strive to create a state of relaxed alertness in students.

Each brain is unique. Teachers should use a variety of strategies that allow students to express visual, auditory, tactile, and emotional preferences in learning. Choices should be available that appeal to individual interests.

> Teachers should use a variety of strategies that allow students to express visual, auditory, tactile, and emotional preferences in learning. Choices should be available that appeal to individual interests.

THE CURRICULUM

A representative from each of the 32 elementary school programs served on the district's elementary curriculum committee in the winter of 1989. The task of this committee, which I chaired, was to set the direction for a smaller task force that would then develop and write the actual curriculum.

The task force drew its 17 members from the elementary curriculum committee and was expanded to include parents and businesspeople. In preparation for writing the curriculum, the task force 1) reviewed the priorities set in *Education 2000: Designing Our Future*, 2) heard testimony from experts in the traditional academic disciplines about core concepts and skills to be included in the new curriculum, 3) reviewed national curriculum reports and current literature calling for integrated curricula, and 4) conducted school-level surveys. The task force met regularly throughout the spring and early summer of 1989 to produce the integrated curriculum, which included as its major components core skills and processes, curriculum strands, major themes and concepts, questions, and unit formats.[5]

Core skills and processes. Skills are considered the core of the curriculum and are seen as essential. The traditional view of basic skills as including only language arts and mathematics is expanded to include thinking skills, physical and sensing skills, and social skills.

Table 1.
Required Major Themes and Concepts, Clustered by Curriculum Strands

Strands	Themes and Concepts					
	Communities	Change	Power	Interactions	Form	Systems
Human Societies	Global community University Diversity Environments Cultures Institutions Heritage Rules/laws Inhabitants Ethnicity	Cycles Adaptation Sociopolitical movements Cause and effect Migration	Authority Force Conflict Influence Use of power	Interdependence Competition Cooperation Survival Needs Wants Communication	Aesthetics Historical perspectives Design principles	Natural systems Created systems Organizational systems Functional systems Institutions Families U.S. government Symbol systems Alphabetical systems Number systems Musical notation
The Earth and the Universe	Ecosystems Environment Inhabitants Balance Intervention	Cycles Adaptation Cause and effect	Energy Force	Interdependence Competition Survival Human intervention Balance	Matter Energy	Natural systems Ecosystems Created systems Organizational systems Functional systems
The Individual	Participation Roles Citizenship Democratic ideals Rights Responsibilities	Growth Life cycle Wellness Dependence/independence HIV/AIDS Substance abuse Cause and effect	Conflict Leadership Influence Use of power	Interdependence Independence	Patterns Aesthetics Basic elements Media Style	Created systems Natural systems Body systems

Source: Betty Jean Eklund Shoemaker, *Education 2000: District 4J Integrated Curriculum and Planning Guide, K-5*, 2nd ed. (Eugene, Ore.: School District 4J, Eugene Public Schools, 1990).

In addition to discrete skills in each of these areas, the curriculum recognizes processes that represent the use of skills in combination. Examples include reading, writing, problem solving, critical and creative thinking, performing, and working in cooperative groups. The Education 2000 Integrated Curriculum specifies a total of 132 core skills.[6]

Curriculum strands and themes. In order to remedy the overcrowded and fragmented nature of Eugene's previous curriculum, the task force decided to devise an organizing principle other than the traditional subject disciplines. The new curriculum is organized into three curriculum strands: "Human Societies," "The Earth and the Universe," and "The Individual."

The "Human Societies" strand—which includes some aspects of the traditional content areas of social studies, health education, and the arts—reflects the richness of diverse cultures and the dignity of all peoples. Students look at themselves as members of an increasingly interdependent, global community and come to feel responsible for its future.

"The Earth and the Universe" strand provides a framework for the content associated with physical, earth, and life sciences, as well as aspects of social studies, health, and art. Content is examined from historical, ethical, and aesthetic perspectives. This strand focuses on the responsibility for understanding, preserving, and managing our planet.

"The Individual" strand emphasizes self-awareness through an understanding of the physical, social, emotional, and creative aspects of each individual. Experiences that integrate these components lead students to develop a sense of self-worth, to engage in creative self-expression, and to become more responsible decision makers. Traditional content areas associated with this strand are the visual and performing arts, physical education, health, literature, and affective education.

Major themes. The three curriculum strands are further subdivided into six themes: communities, change, power, interactions, form, and systems. Each of these themes serves as an umbrella concept under which many related concepts are clustered. Table 1 shows the specific topics generated by the curriculum strands and themes.

Questions. Questions play an important role in the development of a concept-based curriculum. Questioning serves its traditional function as an important strategy for fostering students' thinking and learning. In the Education 2000 Integrated Curriculum, questions also serve as a planning tool for teachers. Teachers use questions to define major themes and to focus selected activities so that they teach the concept or theme intended. The curriculum guide provides key words to assist teachers in developing appropriate questions related to concepts and themes.

> **A prescribed set of steps for planning a unit ensures that the integrating theme is explicit and that there is a clear link between the theme and the core concepts and skills to be taught.**

Unit development. The curriculum framework of strands and themes provides some flexibility in the way that units are developed. The Eugene Public Schools operate on a three-term school year. One way of allocating the time is to cover one curriculum strand (exploring all six themes) each term. Other programs develop units that cover the six major conceptual themes over the course of one year; each thematic unit is taught over a six-week period and deals with all three curriculum strands within the six weeks.

A prescribed set of steps for planning a unit ensures that the integrating theme is explicit and that there is a clear link between the theme and the core concepts and skills to be taught. The steps in developing and implementing a unit are:

1. Select major themes and concepts. Teachers identify the broad focus of the unit and brainstorm for possible topics and skills related to this theme. They identify strengths, interests, and misconceptions.

2. Generate a list of questions related to the concepts and theme. The answers to these questions should identify the core knowledge and skills that students need to master by the end of the unit. Later, teachers plan unit activities geared specifically to helping students answer the questions (which are posted in the room before beginning the unit).

3. Narrow the focus. Teachers select the strongest possibilities from the brainstormed list, which may include those topics and skills that form natural relationships within the theme, that fulfill required curriculum standards, or that can be developed with available materials and resources. Teachers then

begin collecting materials and resources that will complement the unit.

4. Begin completing the skills chart. Teachers identify both those skills that students will need to start the unit and those that can be taught as the unit progresses. They provide ample opportunity for students to apply newly learned skills within meaningful contexts as opposed to relying on rote drills. Some skills will be selected because they naturally lend themselves to the theme. Others will be chosen because they are important for students to learn at that level; thus a context will be created within the unit to teach them.

5. Develop daily plans and add appropriate instructional materials. Teachers plan the unit so that the "big picture" is presented at the beginning, and movement occurs freely between the big picture and the pieces throughout the unit. Teachers also select activities that address student learning styles, that require the use of a variety of strategies, and that help students make direct connections to the major theme and concepts being explored. Developmentally appropriate practices keep students actively engaged and increase their understanding of how the new knowledge relates to previously learned material.

6. Identify possible products and assessment strategies, which will take a variety of forms and can reflect both quantitative and qualitative measures. Teachers engage individual students in answering the questions and prod students to translate declarative knowledge into applied knowledge through the development of student-selected projects.

7. Teach the unit.

8. Evaluate student progress and revise the unit as appropriate.

IMPLEMENTATION

The Education 2000 Integrated Curriculum is in its second year of development and implementation. The initial stages of implementation involved open communication between teachers and administrators and the training (in the fall of 1989) of approximately 90 teachers who volunteered to participate in a pilot study. At the end of that academic year, the curriculum was correlated with Oregon's Essential Learning Skills and

Common Curriculum Goals, changes were made, and a revised edition was published.

Representatives of each elementary program—including parents, principals, and teachers—received a three-hour orientation to the curriculum in the fall of 1989. Various staff development opportunities were later made available in individual schools. These ranged from brief introductions to the curriculum to elaborate schoolwide training sessions on how to plan units. Teachers also receive training in interpersonal communication, decision-making processes, and team building. In addition, overviews of the curriculum are presented to parent groups at both the district and school levels.

> From a teaching standpoint, it's a lot more fun. It gives the teacher more control over the depth of study of topics that are being explored.

District-level staff development classes are offered in the theoretical foundations of integrative education and in curriculum development. As thematic instructional units are developed, the district's instructional materials center coordinates their dissemination.

What do teachers think of the new curriculum? Nancy McCullum, a fourth-grade teacher at Bailey Hill Elementary School, commented: "From a teaching standpoint, it's a lot more fun. It gives the teacher more control over the depth of study of topics that are being explored. Students get to look at something from a lot of different angles. They really like it. So far, we have had good responses from both parents and children. The projects that they do at home have been a big factor in that."

From an administrative point of view, the implementation of the curriculum has been facilitated by a number of factors. Martha Harris, the director of curriculum and instruction for the district, noted: "The Education 2000 Integrated Curriculum works well in our district, where sites have a long tradition of decentralized decision making. Our schools have a history of being responsive to their communities through the development of programs that best suit the needs of their own students." Moreover, there has been no pressure from the central office for schools to implement the curriculum immediately.

The model is not without problems, however. "The biggest problem is planning time," said McCullum. "I think that, after a few years, when we've got a core of developed units, this will take care of itself." In addition, some teachers find it difficult to adjust to being members of a team, while matters of assessment and gaining the support of parents present their own problems.

In general, though, the program has met with a positive response. The comments of Michelle Markus, the media specialist at Edgewood Elementary School, reveal the beneficial effect the curriculum has already had on both teachers and students: "The integrated curriculum is a great gift to experienced teachers. It's like getting a new pair of lenses that make teaching a lot more exciting and help us look forward into the next century. It is helping students take control of their own learning."

NOTES

1. Anne C. Lewis, "Getting Unstuck: Curriculum as a Tool of Reform, " *Phi Delta Kappan*, March 1990, p. 534-538.

2. Some of the material included in this article was originally published in Betty Jean Eklund Shoemaker, "Integrative Education: A Curriculum for the Twenty-First Century," *Oregon School Study Council Bulletin*, vol. 33, 1989. For a copy of this publication, send $6 to the Oregon School Study Council, 1787 Agate St., University of Oregon, Eugene, OR 97403.

3. Martha J. Harris, ed., *Education 2000: Designing Our Future* (Eugene, Ore.: Preliminary Report of the Elementary Study Committee, School District 4J, Eugene Public Schools, 1988).

4. Renate N. Caine and Geoffrey Caine, "Understanding a Brain-Based Approach to Learning and Teaching," *Educational Leadership*, October 1990, p. 66-70.

5. Betty Jean Eklund Shoemaker, *Education 2000: District 4J Integrated Curriculum and Planning Guide, K-5*, 2nd ed. (Eugene, Ore.: School District 4J, Eugene Public Schools, 1990).

6. In developing the list of required skills, the task force drew on Robert Marzano et al., *Dimensions of Thinking: A Framework for Curriculum and Instruction* (Alexandria, Va.: Association for Supervision and Curriculum Development, 1988); Hill Walker, *The Walker Social Skills Curriculum: The ACCEPTS Program* (Austin, Tex.: Pro-Ed, 1988); and David Johnson et al., *Circles of Learning: Cooperation in the Classroom* (Alexandria, Va.: Association for Supervision and Curriculum Development, 1984).

Integrated Learning: Ideas in Practice

"The ground itself is moving," [Emory 1969]: our underlying frames, gestalts, paradigms, big pictures are everywhere in doubt. The task is to understand how we acquire frames, how we communicate them, and how we change them in ourselves and others.— Peter Vail, *Management as a Performing Art*, 1989, p. 106

Sometimes the best way to effect change is to possess an image of what that change looks like. The transition toward more connected, more holistic learning is eased when teachers can imagine what integrative learning actually looks like. Once teachers grasp the concept, their energy and creativity carries them the rest of the way as they engage in their labor of love. As one team explained, "Integrating the curricula is like spaghetti because the more you get into it, the harder it is to get out; it's so entangling!"

Perhaps the most dramatic way to expose teachers to integrated curricula is to demonstrate with specific examples that illustrate exactly what some teachers are doing in their classrooms. Thus, Section 5 provides four distinct curriculum integration ideas that are in practice today.

Webster describes an idea that has gained much favor from the primary grades to the graduate school of design and engineering: "Projects as Curriculum." Elements to consider as one implements a project orientation curriculum design include managing levels of involvement, use of basic skills and construction of knowledge for each learner.

Three teachers show how to connect curriculum with concrete examples used in their own classrooms. In a unit called, "Towers of Spaghetti," Foster gives a step-by-step account of a tower project showing how language arts, social studies, math, and science are structured into an engineering challenge for sixth graders.

In "Play Ball," Konar demonstrates how to use simple baseball cards to teach math facts, inspire reading and writing activities, and spark interest in mapping, geography, and history with students. Brumbaugh details how to integrate the curriculum when studying Pilgrims with second graders. "Setting Sail—The Pilgrims' Voyage" tells how students practice geography, science, and language arts skills in a mock journey across the ocean.

Maute's hierarchy of cross-curricular connections delineates a model that includes the incident, the activity, the arrangement, the assignment, the unit, and the event. Using this plan, teachers become aware of those "teachable moments" in which a cross-curricular connection can be exploited.

Authors Smith and Johnson explain how to integrate the curricula at the middle school level offering five components to create a successful integrative literature unit. "Bringing It Together: Literature in an Integrative Curriculum," details the stages of planning step by step.

These articles focus on specific integrated learning episodes that give some glimpses into that classroom or schoolhouse where holistic education is happening.

Projects as Curriculum: Under What Conditions?

by Tupper Webster

With increasing frequency, current discussion about early childhood curriculum content and methods includes references to project work by children. There is even a tendency to equate the use of projects to providing a developmentally appropriate curriculum. Of particular concern to this writer is the use of projects as appealing "specials," tucked into the schedule among an unrelated practice-as-usual curriculum. All too often projects become something children do *after* reading and math skills have been taught and drilled, with little effect on basic classroom instruction.

The use of projects as a means of enhancing children's learning is commonly viewed as more informal and far less structured than the usual teacher-directed lessons focused on specific content or skills. When used, projects may reflect children's interests or may be imposed by the teacher who views them as being age-appropriate. Teacher-originated projects prevail in many classrooms. Every fall children reenact the first Thanksgiving by building the Mayflower in the block area, making Pilgrims' hats and Indian headbands during art, "performing" the play for parents and helping prepare a Thanksgiving dinner. February finds a "post office" constructed in the block area and valentines "mailed" to classmates. While such familiar projects can spark

> With increasing frequency, current discussion about early childhood curriculum content and methods includes references to project work by children.

From *Childhood Education*, vol. 67, no. 1, p. 2-3, Fall 1990.
Reprinted with permission.

children's interests enough to extend their involvement and learning, there should be distinct variations each year tailored to the particular group of children.

Advocates of a project curriculum that is developmentally appropriate and meaningful acknowledge that "doing" projects is not a new idea in early childhood education. The Bank Street model, the Plowden Report and British Infant Schools, "Open Education," the Piagetian-based curriculum, Dewey's ideas on thematic activities, Carolyn Pratt's discoveries about children's learning, hands-on science teaching—all these and more from early education's rich heritage reflect aspects or features that are in effect when children engage in project learning. Certainly, like project work, all place the child at the center of curricular practice.

The sandbox, woodworking bench, water area, art and writing materials, blocks, math/science items, all kinds of books, library and media supplies, trips and resource people become the wherewithal to create and carry out projects arising from children's interests or from questions posed by teachers. When a group of 1st-graders chose to delve into Japanese culture, they experienced activities ranging from doll-making to interpretive dance to comparing folktales to discovery of shared human qualities; an integrated curriculum resulted, emphasizing individualized and shared learning (Golver, 1990). Eight-year-olds in another classroom, engaged in learning about knights and castles, moved from sand castle construction to books about life in the Middle Ages, then back to the sand table, art materials and wood working to construct details of medieval environments (Barbour, Webster & Drosdeck, 1987).

The appropriateness of projects in the school curriculum is not limited to the primary grades. Secondary students in Rabun County, Georgia, began taking responsibility for their own bulletin board, then moved to writing and publishing their own magazine. They wrote articles about people and practices of the surrounding community, based on interviews with local citizens. Less well known than the ultimate success of their *Foxfire Magazine* is the impact on their young lives of the very individualized but shared teaching and learning made available to them. First viewed as alienated by school, the students gradually undertook with confidence and vitality the academic work of research and writing, but only after it was *perceived by them* as having personal meaning and value (Wigginton, 1985). Projects in the *Foxfire* tradition engage students in meaningful learning. Advance planning by students and teachers remains flexible as the project work progresses and results in activities requiring sustained effort by individual students or groups of students over several days or weeks.

Most children enjoy projects that engage them in learning, unlike the practice and drill of worksheets. But are the projects developed in response to children's questions? Do the projects give rise to children's independent, creative thinking? Are they managed in ways that enable diverse levels of involvement and diverse cognitive challenges so that no child is forced to see him/herself as a failure? Are there features within the scope of the project that invite—necessitate—the use of basic academic skills? Is there room for all participants to experience both social cooperation and moral responsibility in order to ensure successful completion of the project? Will participation provide possibilities for children to increase their knowledge and appreciation of the "stuff of their world"—materials, objects, people, events? Do the projects reflect children's attempts to construct their own understanding and interpretations?

> Most children enjoy projects that engage them in learning, unlike the practice and drill of worksheets.

Obviously, the actual value of any project for a child or group of children depends upon some very complex considerations. A sprinkling of projects across the year, month or day is of limited value; to encourage, permit or require projects that have little relationship to the remainder of the curriculum is not enough. A teacher's view of the way children learn, what they can or should learn, and the values reflected in procedures and relationships within the classroom are crucial determinants of the wise use of projects. These views should be consistently evident throughout the school day in all facets of the group life.

If a teacher's decisions about math or reading instruction are essentially determined on the basis of grade level assessments or a highly structured, predetermined curriculum for all children, the use of projects is philosophically proscribed.

Teachers must be allowed to express enough faith in children to use projects as a source of valid learning, or they will continue to convey to children that schooling only means achieving high marks on facts and skills that educators have parceled out in grade level packages.

Furthermore, if projects are simply an added feature of the "academic" curriculum, the teacher will have little motivation to undertake the challenge of this kind of teaching or opportunity to experience the delights and rewards inherent in it. Guiding, facilitating, enabling project work—these are mere words unless actual practice finds the teacher fully aware of reasons for starting, expanding, altering, influencing project work of children. The teacher must look for answers to such questions as: Which projects for which children? What does a given child or group of children already know as a foundation or starting point? What meaningful learning is possible for this child within the realm of a given project? What resources, attitudes, questions should I bring to the project? What features of the child's involvement can reveal growth, and how is this growth to be assessed?

Meaningful use of projects necessitates knowledgeable, thinking, reflective teachers with the autonomy to make intellectually honest curricular decisions in the best interest of each child.

REFERENCES AND RESOURCES

Barbour, N., Webster, T.C., & Drosdeck, S. (1987). Sand: A resource for the language arts. *Young Children, 42* (3), 20-25.

Bredekamp, S. (1987). *Developmentally appropriate practice in early childhood programs serving children from birth through age 8.* Washington, DC: National Association for the Education of Young Children.

Copple, C., Sigel, I.E., & Saunders, R. (1979). *Educating the young thinker: Classroom strategies for cognitive growth.* New York: D. Van Nostrand.

Gamberg, R. et al. with G. Edwards. (1988). *Learning and living it: Theme studies in the classroom.* Portsmouth, NH: Heinemann.

Glover, M.K. (1990). A bag of hair: American 1st-graders experience Japan. *Childhood Education, 66,* 155-159.

Hirsch, E.S. (Ed.).(1984). *The block book.* Washington, DC: National Association for the Education of Young Children.

Katz, L.G., & Chard, S.C. (1989). *Engaging children's minds: The project approach.* Norwood, NJ: Ablex.

Piaget, J. (1973). *To understand is to invent: The future of education.* New York: Grossman Publishers.

Pratt, C. (1948, 1970). *I learn from children,* New York: Harper & Row.

San José, C. (1989). Classroom drama: Learning from the inside out. In S. Hoffman & L.L. Lamme (Eds.), *Learning from the inside out: The expressive arts* (p. 69-76). Wheaton, MD: Association for Childhood Education International.

Seefeldt, C., & Barbour, N. (1990). *Early childhood education: An introduction.* Columbus, OH: Merrill.

Wigginton, E. (1985). *Sometimes a shining moment: The Foxfire experience.* Garden City, NY: Anchor Press/Doubleday.

Connect Your Curriculum

by Andrea Foster, Shayne Konar, and Allyne Brumbaugh

[Three] teachers show you how with integrated units that make sense of the disciplines

Towers of Spaghetti

by Andrea Foster

What do ping-pong balls, marshmallows, spaghetti sticks, and imagination add up to? Tall towers—and interdisciplinary activities guaranteed to get students applying creativity and scientific process skills to solve real-world problems of engineering and design.

I begin this unit by showing my students a picture of the Leaning Tower of Pisa. I encourage them to speculate as to why the tower leans before we discuss the real reason—an inadequate foundation set upon poor soil. Students learn more about the tower by researching its beginnings and its future: Who built it? How far will it lean? Will it eventually fall over, be demolished, or be preserved? Finally, students take on their own engineering challenge—building tall towers of spaghetti. Here's how we do it.

PREPARE TO BUILD

You will need plenty of miniature marshmallows (left uncovered overnight so they are slightly stale), uncooked spaghetti sticks (approximately one package per class), one roll of masking tape, and several ping-pong balls. Set a price for each material, for example, a stick of spaghetti might cost $100, an inch of masking tape $10, and marshmallows $50 each. Designate an area of the classroom as the building-supply headquarters and stock the store with the supplies.

Excerpted from *Instructor* magazine, vol. 101, no. 2, p. 24-32, September 1991. Reprinted with permission.

Divide the class into teams of several students each and give each team a ping-pong ball. Tell students that they will be given fifteen minutes to construct the tallest and cheapest tower possible. Teams must follow these rules:

1. The tower must be built as high as possible, and when finished, must support the ping-pong ball.

2. Any amount of materials may be "purchased" from the "Building Supply Headquarters" according to the posted price list.

3. Once purchased, materials may not be returned for a refund.

4. After the construction period, the height of each structure will be measured from the base of the tower to the top of the ball.

5. The structure must remain standing by itself after construction with the ping-pong ball on top.

6. The ping-pong ball cannot be damaged or altered during or after construction.

7. The height of the tower and the total cost of materials will determine team score.

For judging purposes, create a Tower Evaluation Sheet (see sample).

Tower Evaluation Sheet

Criteria	Possible Points	Earned Points
TOWER HEIGHT		
1'-0" to 1'-6"	20	____
1'-7" to 2'-0"	40	____
2'-1" to 2'-6"	60	____
2'-7" to 3'-0"	80	____
Over 3'-0"	100	____
Tower Height ___		
COST OF MATERIALS		
up to $500	50	____
$501-$700	40	____
$701-$900	30	____
$901-$1100	20	____
$1101-$1300	10	____
Over $1300	0	____
Material $1300	0	____
Material Cost ____		
CONSTRUCTION TECHNIQUES		
Durability	30	____
Neatness	30	____
TOTAL	200	____

THE BUILDING BEGINS

Have students meet in groups to plan architectural strategies. Give each team time to purchase materials then let the 15-minute building time begin.

When 15 minutes are up, have each group stop building and share their results. Have teams describe their designs and explain how they chose materials and built their towers. Encourage them to tell of any snags in the construction process. Would they do anything differently the second time around? Compare and contrast towers. Are any similar in design? Distribute copies of the Tower Evaluation Sheet and have teams tabulate their own results.

BUILDING ON A THEME

Take advantage of the fun and excitement generated by this building activity by integrating the idea with the other subjects you teach.

Language Arts

Use a camera to preserve your Towers of Spaghetti experience. Photograph the construction process and the final products. Pass out the developed photographs to students and have them use the pictures to write real estate advertisements in which they try to sell their towers, or write tourist brochures in which they describe the towers' attractions to visitors.

Careers, Social Studies, Art

Use the building experience as a springboard to having students learn more about building design and construction:

• Provide students with copies of architectural magazines. Take a neighborhood walk, notice the variety of building constructions and designs, and compare them with building details represented in the magazines.

• Call a local architecture firm and request discarded blueprints for students to examine. Have them sketch a finished version of the structure based on the blueprint.

• Have students research famous structures such as the Statue of Liberty in New York, the Sears Tower in Chicago, or the TransAmerica Pyramid in San Francisco. Do their designs have anything in common?

• Make a map of your neighborhood highlighting distinctive buildings—the tallest, shortest, oldest, most unusual, and so on. Research the buildings' architects and builders. Were any buildings designed by the same person or firm? If so, do the buildings' designs reflect similarities in architectural style?

Math/Science

Build the ultimate tower of spaghetti with this exercise in cooperative learning. Have students identify design highlights of each tower constructed. Which features contributed to effective designs? Which contributed to ineffective designs? Discuss advantages and disadvantages of expensive structures versus less-costly structures. Have students apply their observations in first designing, and then constructing the tallest, least expensive tower of them all.

Play Ball!

by Shayne Konar

Turn baseball cards into a tool for teaching, and your classroom into a field of dreams

Want to hit a home run with your students this year? Look no further than the nearest stack of baseball cards.

MATH

The backs of baseball cards explode with math facts. When you use baseball statistics to reinforce computational skills and to introduce new operations, students will discover natural relationships between math and one of their favorite hobbies.

• Group cards according to teams, players' positions, length of players' careers, home runs hit in a single year, players' birth dates and places, and hands used to bat and throw. Try graphing some of the information, for example, to show home runs hit in a single year by different teams, or home runs hit by players in different age ranges (21-23, 23-25, and so on).

• Rank players by the number of home runs earned or games played.

• Estimate how many cards are in a given stack. Estimate how many cards set end-to-end would equal the length of a bat (or a baseball glove or a cap). How many would reach around a baseball diamond? Find out the actual number of cards for each estimate given.

• Calculate the average number of times a player has a chance to hit the ball in a game by dividing the number of games played by the number of times up at bat.

SOCIAL STUDIES

Baseball cards provide plenty of information for mapping, geography, and history activities:

• Guess the state that sends the most players to the big leagues. The fewest? Check your answers by mapping where players were born.

• Post a map of the United States on a bulletin board. Use colorful pushpins to indicate baseball landmarks. Use a different color pushpin to represent each landmark category.

• Find the shortest highway route that links the teams' cities in one division.

• Use a map and a team's playing schedule (get this from the team headquarters) to calculate the total distance a team travels during a season. How does that distance compare with the distances other teams travel?

• Make a time line showing historical moments in baseball.

• Create a picture report on equipment and uniform changes throughout the history of baseball.

• Graph the history of the World Series. First, ask students to guess which league, the American or National, has won more World Series. Which division (Eastern or Western) of each league has played in and won more World Series? After researching the facts, graph this bit of baseball history.

ART

Put students' creative energies to work with these activities:

• Redesign a baseball emblem, or create a new emblem for a local or fictious team.

• Create personalized stat-packed baseball cards: Photocopy photographs of each student. Trim each picture to fit on the front of an index card, and glue in place. Have students each record personal data on the back of their cards. Laminate cards, or cover front and back of cards with clear adhesive paper.

LANGUAGE ARTS

Baseball cards can inspire reading and writing excitement in your classroom:

• Breathe life into inanimate objects by writing about a day in the life of a bat, baseball, or glove. So essays will have an authentic ring, incorporate real-life statistics (from the cards) into the writings.

• Craft player biographies from the statistics and profiles that appear on the backs of the cards and from research on a player's life.

• Create a classroom library featuring trade books about baseball. Invite students to bring in their favorite baseball books and to spend time in the library selecting others. *Frank and Ernest Play Ball!* by Alexandra Day (Scholastic, 1990), and *All About Baseball* by George Sullivan (Putnam, 1989) are two to get you started.

THE FINAL INNING

Bring your baseball unit home by focusing on the hobby of collecting. Brainstorm a list of the possible reasons people collect items such as baseball cards. Have students interview friends and family members to generate a list of likely and unlikely collectibles.

Talk about baseball cards that have become rare and valuable. (For example, a Honus Wagner card recently sold for $450,000. Wagner cards are rare because Wagner stopped the presses when he found out the cards bore a cigarette advertisement.) Ask students to discuss how something could be of great value to one person, but have little or no value someone else. Have students speculate what will become valuable in their lifetimes.

etting Sail—The Pilgrims' Voyage

by Allyne Brumbaugh

Don't wait until Thanksgiving to introduce your students to the Pilgrims—set sail in September!

When my second-graders arrive on September 5th, they see a bulletin-board display of the Mayflower. On September 6th they set sail for America—the same day, 370 years ago, that the Pilgrims began their journey. We don't complete our journey until December, but along the way we integrate history with science, math, geography, and language arts.

I introduce the unit with some background information on the Pilgrims and their journey. We discuss the Pilgrims' reasons for leaving England, including the need to seek a better life and to escape religious persecution. (Actually, only about 35 of the 102 passengers were seeking religious freedom).

When we're ready to sail, I put on an inexpensive captain's hat to make the transformation from teacher to Master Christopher Jones, Captain of the Mayflower. I wear the hat whenever I want the class to know that we are "aboard the Mayflower."

Ready to put on your Captain's hat? Details, including real Pilgrim children's names for your students to adopt, follow.

THE EXPEDITION

As your students travel from England to America, incorporate the following activities to broaden students' learning in all the subject areas.

Geography

Ready your classroom for Pilgrim studies with a bulletin-board display depicting the Mayflower en route to America. Begin by covering a large board with blue craft paper. Obtain a large, discarded map of the world and trim apart the continents of North America, South America, Europe, and Africa. Staple these to the board. If you are unable to find a map to cut apart, or if your map features continents that are too small in size for your bulletin board, trace and cut out continents from a small scale map and enlarge them using an overhead projector. Complete the display with construction-paper ocean waves (or draw waves onto the blue craft paper with a dark blue or black marker).

Have students use a world map to label the continents and the ocean. Have them mark the Mayflower's departure and destination sites, draw a line between them to represent its route, and divide the route into 66 equal parts (representing the 66 days of the voyage). Tack an oaktag Mayflower replica to the shores of England and have students take turns each day moving the ship one increment closer to its destination of Plymouth, Massachusetts. Use the display to acquaint students with geographical terms such as *peninsula, bay, coastline,* as well as points of interest along the northeastern seaboard of the United States.

The Pilgrim Children

Boys	*Girls*
Bartholomew Allerton	Mary Allerton
John Billington	Remember Allerton
Francis Billington	Mary Chilton
Love Brewster	Humility Cooper
Wrasling Brewster	Constance Hopkins
John Cook	Damaris Hopkins
John Crakston	Desire Minter
Samuel Fuller	Ellen More
Giles Hopkins	Patricia Mullins
William Latham	Elizabeth Tilley

From *Alphabetical List of Passengers on the Mayflower,* available from Plimouth Museum, Plimouth Plantation, Box 1620, Plymouth, MA 02360; (508)746-1622 (send $1.25 and a business-size SASE).

Science

During the voyage, acquaint students with the importance of checking and recording weather conditions. Show students how to read a weather thermometer. Have them record their observations on a bulletin-board-size temperature graph. Keep a class journal in which children record precipitation and sky conditions.

After gathering information for a month, have children refer to their data to answer questions such as, "Which two consecutive days had the greatest change in temperature?" and "How do the temperatures for the second week of September compare with those for the second week of October?" Challenge students to record predictions regarding temperature and weather conditions and then compare actual temperatures and conditions.

Language Arts
From preparing for their journey to arriving at their destination, students will have plenty to think about. Have them record their thoughts in journals, taking on the identity of an actual Pilgrim child as they write (see list of children's names). During your journey, encourage students to make frequent entries, beginning, for example, with what they will miss most about their homeland and what they hope will be different in America. By simulating actual diaries the Pilgrim children may have kept, students have a chance to craft their own historical fiction.

Read aloud voyage-related literature. Books such as *Why the Tides Ebb and Flow* by Joan Chase Bowden (Houghton Mifflin, 1990), *Watch the Stars Come Out* by Riki Levenson (E.P. Dutton, 1985), and *How Many Days To America?* by Eve Bunting (Clarion, 1990) help children incorporate the emotional and scientific impact of this incredible journey into their writings.

THE NEW WORLD
Celebrate landing your cardboard Mayflower with a discussion of what life must have been like for the Pilgrims in Plymouth. For a realistic look at life on an early-American settlement, read *Sara Morton's Day* by Kate Waters (Scholastic, 1989). Then, have students conclude their own journals with first-person accounts of their own lives as Pilgrim children in the New World.

Cross-Curricular Connections

by Joan Maute

Opportunities abound to correlate, fuse, integrate separate subjects and areas. The author presents a way of looking at these "connections" and some reasons for capitalizing on them.

One of the great advantages of interdisciplinary teams is the opportunity it gives teachers to integrate learning among various subjects. This intertwining of subject matter not only reinforces what is taught, but also more closely resembles life outside the classroom where the subjects we teach are not found in isolation, but, rather, are constantly interacting with and overlapping each other. As a teacher in a school that made the transition from a departmentalized structure to one with interdisciplinary teams, I found that we were constantly bombarded with information about something called "I.D.U." Once we realized that this was *not* a form of birth control but an Interdisciplinary Unit, (a unit of study that looks at one subject or topic through many disciplines) we were excited about creating and implementing our own I.D.U.'s—and became believers.

Teams at our school engage in many I.D.U.'s each year, and they never fail to get students involved with and enthusiastic about the topic. Because of the success of these units I believe we need to look more closely for ways to integrate learning. Perhaps we should put less emphasis on occasional large units and more emphasis on the day-to-day potential that exists for cross-curricular connections. Cross-curricular connections are connections between two or more areas of study that are made by teachers within the structure of their disciplines. Examples could include music and math; art and advisory; En-

From *Middle School Journal*, vol. 20, no. 4, p. 20-22, March 1989. Reprinted with permission.

glish, science, and physical education; and so on. One might think of the middle school curriculum as a pinball machine with the subjects being the bumpers and the teacher being the ball that can help the player (student) win by making connections.

BUT WHY BOTHER?

There are many reasons to use cross-curricular connections. These connections can help us reach students with various learning styles. By using art or music in any of the basic subjects a teacher can appeal to visual and auditory learners. The kinetic learning inherent in classes such as industrial arts and home economics does not have to be limited to just those courses. Food from various countries can be served in a world cultures class, and instruments made in shop can be played in music. Utilizing cross-curricular connections also allows for capitalizing on students' subject preferences. Most students prefer one or more subjects over others; by making cross-curricular connections, the student who dislikes math may find it more palatable when it is applied in a favorite social studies or English class.

> Cross-curricular connections are connections between two or more areas of study that are made by teachers within the structure of their disciplines.

Students can apply what is learned in one area to another area of study much more readily when teachers make cross-curricular connections. Such applications give learning greater meaning as the original learning is reinforced and the new learning becomes more familiar. In some cases cross-curricular connections can help bridge the gap between theory and practice. Through seeing cross-curricular relationships, students can begin to realize that learning, like life, is not a spectator sport.

MAUTE'S HIERARCHY OF CROSS-CURRICULAR CONNECTIONS

As you might guess, there are many levels and examples of cross-curricular connections. At the base of this hierarchy is what I like to call the *cross-curricular incident*. The incident can happen more frequently than other types of connections. It is very simple and, once mastered, becomes so natural that students and teachers take it for granted. An incident happens when a social studies teacher, who knows the English teacher is teaching adjectives, asks the students for adjectives to describe a country, civilization, landform, or event. Incidents occur when math teachers compare fractions to music notes or when art teachers talk of proportions used to mix colors. You can see how the list of incidents could go on forever, and right now I'm sure you can think of cross-curricular incidents that are happening or could be happening all the time in your subject.

> Any activity that happens within a class and incorporates two or more subject areas can be classified as a cross-curricular activity.

The next step up from the incident is the *cross-curricular activity*. I play a game in sixth-grade social studies called Silent World. This game is a modification of that elementary favorite, Silent Ball. In Silent World students sit on their desks and gently (I always remind them to be gentle with our world) toss an inflatable globe from student to student. The room is completely silent except when a student catches the world. When the student catches the world, he or she must tell the class what continent or ocean his or her right thumb is on or closest to. I have one globe that also has animals placed on their home continent or ocean. In that game students name the animal as well as the continent or ocean. If they miss the world or talk out of turn, they become a spectator, not participants in the game. This activity incorporates reading, social studies, science, and physical education as the students become aware of the relative locations of oceans, continents, and animals while practicing the study skills of listening and following directions.

Music can be used to introduce lessons in social studies (Maute, 1988). Any activity that happens within a class and incorporates two or more subject areas can be classified as a cross-curricular activity. As you think through the last unit you taught you will become aware of the fact that you had some cross-curricular activities. Now think of more you could add as you continue through your present unit.

As we work our way up the hierarchy, we now encounter the *cross-curricular assignment.* This assignment requires the student to do work, either in or out of class, that involves two or more disciplines. When my students were reading *The Phantom Tollbooth,* I copied the map from the inside cover of the book. I drew longitude and latitude lines on the map and asked my students to list the coordinates for Dictionopolis, Digitopolis, the tollbooth, the Doldrums, and other locations in the story. The math teacher expanded the assignment by asking the students to create a scale and measure distances between points on the map. These assignments allowed us to reinforce earlier learnings in our subjects while giving the students a fuller understanding of the land about which they were reading.

> **Writing and performing a "rap" song (Maute, 1987) can help students remember facts as they lead the rest of the class in review.**

When given a choice, students often make their own cross-curricular connections using preferred learning modes. Illustrations can become concrete ways of learning idioms while students practice art in English. Writing and performing a "rap" song (Maute, 1987) can help students remember facts as they lead the rest of the class in review. Concrete learners can build models for science or social studies to show what they have learned. The cross-curricular assignment is very likely already present in many of your school's classes.

We have now worked our way up to the I.D.U., *Interdisciplinary Units* which combine incidents, activities, and assignments. They frequently provide short term, in-depth focus on a specific topic (Kerekes, 1987). It is not unusual for a team to suspend "regular" classes while implementing an interdisciplinary unit. Well-received interdisciplinary units require a lot of planning, energy, and creativity. They provide a break from the usual routine and are thoroughly enjoyed by students and teachers alike. The value of a good interdisciplinary unit cannot be overemphasized. (For more information about interdisciplinary units see the August 1987 *Middle School Journal.*)

At the top of the hierarchy beyond the I.D.U., we find the ultimate cross-curricular connection. This is the *cross-curricular EVENT!* Quite often interdisciplinary units will have a culminating event. Our sixth-grade teams finish their interdisciplinary unit on Greece and Rome with the Greek and Roman Festival. Over the years we have included food prepared by the students, a catapult contest, banners, Olympic events, newspapers, drama, "Meet Our City-State" television programs (Athens A.M. or Troy Today complete with the latest traffic and weather reports), gods and goddesses, and every student in a costume as part of the festival. Students remember these events forever, (Who could forget the sight of 150 sixth-graders in sheets?) but the incidents, activities, assignments, and units make the events possible.

PUTTING IT TOGETHER

There are three major pieces to the cross-curricular puzzle. The first and most important piece is awareness of what is being taught in other classes. Any connection between subject areas is good but if connections are made parallel to each other, they are even better. You cannot make connections with what is going on currently in another class if you do not know what is being taught there. For interdisciplinary teams this information comes in a team meeting. Our team committed one meeting a week for "academic plans." We used this time to schedule tests for the following week and let each other know what we were teaching in both the near and distant future. As time went on, we became more aware of each other's curricula and could work toward more correlation. It is more difficult to become aware of the content being taught outside of your team so some forum should exist to accomplish this. What your students learn in physical education, music, art, shop, home economics, computers, foreign language, and other exploratories especially needs to be connected with the basic subjects.

The second piece of the good cross-curricular puzzle is planning. Once you are aware of curriculum outside of your own, you can work alone or with other teachers to look for connections, and plan incidents, activities, assignments, units, and events that take advantage of this knowledge. The higher up the pyramid you go, the more planning becomes necessary.

The final piece to the puzzle is flexibility. Once you have achieved awareness and planning, you must be willing to fold, bend, stretch, move, and yes, even sometimes leave out part of what you had planned. The results will be more responsive to your students' needs and have more meaning as it fuses new and old learnings in many areas. As you continue to work with these and look for connections, you will see your students beginning to make connections on their own.

Returning to the pinball machine analogy, the more frequently the ball bounces off various bumpers, the higher the score will be. The ball can travel from bumper to bumper for quite a while on its own but not forever. To truly win the game, it becomes necessary for the player to hit the flippers and try to make more connections. True interdisciplinary teaching is ongoing. As teachers we should be striving not only to make connections for our students, but also to teach them to see and make their own connections. When they have connected with learning, applied it in many areas, and revised and revamped their knowledge, they can't help being winners.

REFERENCES

Kerekes, J. (1987, August) The interdisciplinary unit... it's here to stay! *Middle School Journal.* p.12-14.

Maute, J. (1988, January) Rapping and mapping. *Science Scope*, p.44-45

Maute, J. (1987, February) Tune in memory. *Middle School Journal.* p.3-5.

Bringing It Together: Literature in an Integrative Curriculum

by J. Lea Smith & Holly Johnson

This book is realer than anything. —Danny C., Grade 8

How many middle grade students say this about a content textbook? Few, if any, because textbooks are often too difficult for reading and learning. They tend to break knowledge into formal clusters of information that do not encourage reader interest, content acquisition, or meaningful retention. In comparison, narrative texts such as adolescent novels promote student interest and increase learning. Brozo and Tomlinson (1986) contend that narrative texts used skillfully make the curriculum more palatable, comprehensible, and memorable.

Narrative texts also create a more relevant, personal, and individualized learning approach. Beane (1992) says that if students are given the opportunity, they will construct their own meanings to answer questions of personal importance which overlap with the concerns of the world at large. When the middle school curriculum centers around young people with real concerns and questions, an environment for authentic and holistic learning is established. Narrative texts unite the concerns of adolescents with the school curriculum and the world we live in. With this in mind, our goal in this article is two-fold. The first is to provide a model for incorporating adolescent literature into Beane's (1990) integrative curriculum. Our integrative approach uses literature to examine a theme that combines the concerns of adolescents and world issues rather than con-

From *Middle School Journal*, vol. 25, no. 1, p. 3-7, September 1993. Reprinted with permission.

centrating on fragmented, traditional subjects with content textbooks. Our approach creates a curriculum that transcends a cursory study of content concepts. Both integrative, thematic studies and narratives by their very nature encourage students to spend more time focusing on a specific theme or concern in detail. In planning and carrying out thematic units using literature, teachers have the opportunity to bring to life such enduring, but elusive, ideas such as democracy, human dignity, and cultural diversity (Beane, 1990).

> Both integrative, thematic studies and narratives by their very nature encourage students to spend more time focusing on a specific theme or concern in detail.

Our second goal is to provide examples of integrative, thematic literature units. Each example uses a selected middle grades narrative text which highlights a curriculum theme built upon an intersection of personal and social concerns. Each example is then illustrated through an integrative concept web. Skills such as communication, computation, and research, in addition to reflective thinking, problem solving, and searching for completeness and meaning, extend from the thematic core and are developed through instructional activities that go beyond academic disciplines. An integrative curriculum consciously incorporates methods and skills from more than the academic disciplines to teach and examine a central theme, issue, situation or topic. This means that the full range of knowledge, from the sciences to the arts, is involved in providing a comprehensive learning experience for students within a specific time period. The interweaving of theme, concepts, and skills is more effective, since they are neither learned nor used in isolation.

Our approach to organizing an integrative unit begins with selecting a central theme which can be developed through the use of adolescent literature. Using narratives as the primary reading materials in thematic studies creates an atmosphere in which students are motivated to become more actively involved in their learning. While young people seem to be more inclined to read novels, nonfiction reading materials can also be included in thematic units. *Nonfiction for Young Adults: From Delight to Wisdom* (Carter & Abrahamson, 1990) provides an outline for integrating this type of literature into the classroom. Integrating any type of literature into thematic units builds broader perspectives between personal and social concerns, as well as known concepts and future learning.

Narrative texts are particularly valuable in the middle grades. Middle school students often have less trouble reading and understanding narratives, since in elementary school most of them used instructional materials structured predominantly by story grammar, which is a set of expectations for the structure of stories to facilitate comprehension and to improve memory of the text (Mandler & Johnson, 1977). Middle school students have limited experiences with content area textbooks, and quite often the middle school curriculum overlooks the need to bridge "learning to read" and "reading to learn." Using narrative texts in thematic studies addresses this transitional stage in reading maturation when adolescents are acquiring knowledge (Chall, 1982). Narrative text, due to their familiar story organization, allow for greater comprehension and application of knowledge gained through reading.

Acquiring knowledge contained within text requires the reader's active involvement. Using narrative texts with young protagonists provides a context of prior knowledge whereby students may identify and thus begin to understand and assimilate different world views and more complex knowledge (Hillerich, 1987; Shanahan, 1989). With narrative texts, the likelihood of information transference increases (Lynch-Brown, 1990).

> Teachers will need to abandon the labeling of academic subjects and approach the curriculum thematically.

LITERATURE IN AN INTEGRATIVE CURRICULUM

For any integrative literature unit to be successful, at least five components must be addressed. First, in the middle school team concept, each teacher needs to be committed to integrated instruction and willing to cooperate and contribute to the process. In planning instruction, teachers will need to abandon the labeling of academic subjects and approach the curriculum thematically. Second, the team needs a common planning time for discussing the theme of the unit and how the different skills and concepts can be developed and integrated during the instructional period. Third, the team may use special community events such as museum exhibits, art shows or cultural festivals

to organize or enlarge the thematic studies. Fourth, teachers will
need to revise schedules to allow time for activities that develop
as part of the overall unit and forfeit traditional, academic instruction. This means that teachers follow the needs and interests of the students. Finally, since integrative literature units
tend to be student-directed and participatory, teachers need to
recognize that the classroom environment is likely to reflect this
active learning.

Our approach in developing an integrative literature unit is
accomplished most effectively through the following stages:

Stage I: Identify thematic focus

The student members of the team identify issues of concern
through a survey created by the team teachers. The survey
would question students' individual concerns and their concerns with the world. For example, questions may include:
"What is your greatest concern about the world today?"; "If you
could change anything about your world, what would it be?";
"What do you worry about the most?"; and "If you could make
only one wish, what would it be?" The survey results are assessed and placed in thematic clusters. From the identified thematic concerns, students and teachers in collaboration determine the unit theme. For example, if a primary adolescent concern is personal growth and a societal issue is cultural differences, the unit theme could be "Differences." This theme is the
intersection of both issues since cultural differences are reflected
in, and can be compared to, adolescent differences. Other books
that could be used to study differences are *Drift* (Mayne, 1985)
and *The War Between the Classes* (Miklowitz, 1985).

Stage II: Select the narrative text

After the team has chosen the curricular theme to study, the
team teachers select a piece of age-appropriate literature to be
used as the primary text. A narrative text that best explores the
theme is chosen from an assortment of books appropriate for
middle graders. For example, a book which would work well in
addressing such concerns as cultural differences, social norms,
explorations, personal growth, intergenerational friendship, and
group identity is *The Witch of Blackbird Pond* (Speare, 1958).
The theme of differences ties these concerns together (Figure 1).
The setting of this historical narrative is a Puritan colony in

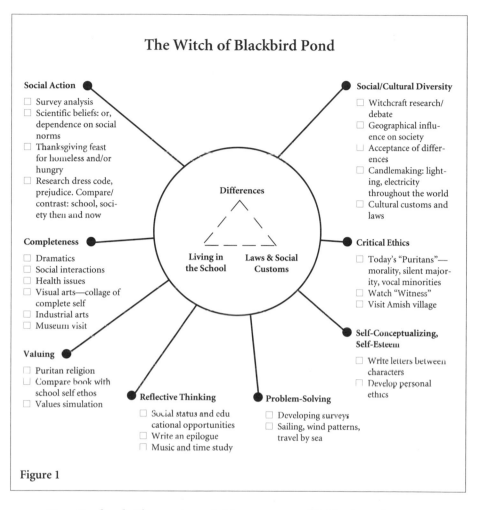

Figure 1

New England. The protagonist is newcomer Kit Taylor, whose colorful clothing and carefree way immediately conflict with the standards of an austere society. Careful depiction of the colony's strict standards of dress and behavior helps readers understand why the Puritans accuse Kit of being a witch (Norton, 1991).

Stage III: Brainstorm and choose study objectives

Students and teachers brainstorm methods and activities that will create a community of learners who explore their concerns and look for answers. At this point, skills are defined, study objectives are discussed and selected, and learning outcomes are determined. The teachers and students become equal participants in the decision-making. For example, in the thematic unit on "Differences," clarifying personal beliefs, behaviors, and decision-making criteria (valuing) could be investigated through a study of societal values involving a survey of parents, grandparents, and other community members. Other skill activities are illustrated on the integrative literature web (Figure 1).

Stage IV: Develop instructional lessons and activities

At this stage, teachers develop instructional strategy lessons that facilitate the students' skill acquisition. These activities are a blend of life skills and the common academic skills of computation, research, and communication. When combined, these skill lessons should eliminate the barriers reflected in a "separatist" curriculum perspective and provide for more authentic learning.

Teachers, instead of being science or language arts or math teachers, cross the subject barriers to create a context for learning in general. Each teacher would use her or his specific knowledge and teaching skills to become a resource and guide all other team members in the activity at hand. In the thematic study of "Differences," one series of skills lessons could relate to surveys: types of surveys; what can be accomplished with surveys; objectives of certain types of surveys; developing and writing up surveys based upon the objectives and types of results desired; administering surveys; and then tabulating, analyzing, and reporting the results. Other activities could help students work through, determine, and analyze their own code of ethics. Comparing values with those espoused in *The Witch of Blackbird Pond* (Speare, 1958) would integrate the knowledge of surveys and the skills of critical ethics, self-concepts, and values.

Creating a unit timeline or calendar that reflects the unit's scope and sequence can be beneficial at this stage. Typically, units range from three to six weeks in duration.

> Before implementing the unit, teachers and students need to identify unit outcomes, assessment strategies, and student evaluations.

Stage V: Establish the evaluation criteria

Before implementing the unit, teachers and students need to identify unit outcomes, assessment strategies, and student evaluations. This ensures that skill objectives will be met, that lesson objectives correlate with evaluation outcomes, and that the unit is evaluated on the material that has been covered. It also would allow formative evaluation of the unit itself, so additional experiences can be designed if objectives are not being met by the unit as initially developed.

Stage VI: Logistics
Next, the team collects and organizes the resources and materials needed for the instructional activities of the unit. This is also the time when a division of labor may benefit the team's goals. That is, one team member becomes responsible for organizing field trips, another the culminating activity, while a third may be responsible for material acquisition. The time needed for planning may vary depending on the book chosen, the length of the unit, and instructional skill activities developed. Our experience suggests that the team should complete unit planning at least one month prior to implementation. This typically provides adequate time for each teacher to follow through on her or his part of the logistics.

INTEGRATED LITERATURE UNIT EXAMPLES
To illustrate how this type of planning might result in a variety of units, we now provide examples of integrated literature units using webs that reflect the unit's central themes. Suggested lessons to be taught for each skill are listed (Figures 2, 3 & 4).

Z for Zachariah, by Robert C. O'Brien
Ann Burden is sixteen and, as far as she knows, the only person left in the world. Through some weather phenomenon, the nuclear radiation that destroyed the rest of the world has not touched the valley where Ann lives. For one year Ann has survived in the valley, farming and living off supplies from the local general store. Then smoke from a distant campfire shatters Ann's solitude. John Loomis, a scientist protected from the radiation by a "safe-suit," makes his way to the valley. John immediately asserts his will, which eventually leads to a confrontation between him and Ann. Ann must choose how she will live, in a world unlike any she has known.

> Themes: Nuclear war, effects of radiation, survival, resourcefulness, dealing with solitude, confrontation, right and wrong, deci-

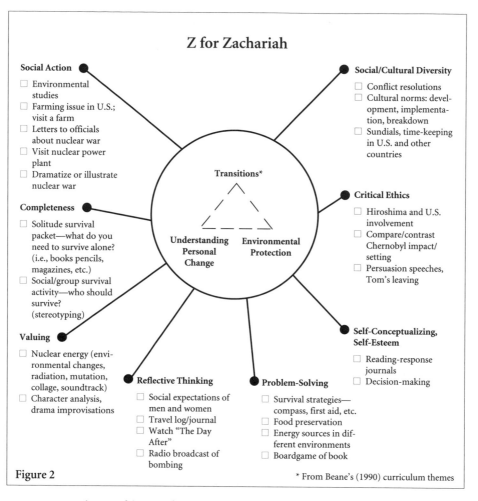

Figure 2

* From Beane's (1990) curriculum themes

sion-making, and expected behaviors. A suggested central theme could be: Transitions. Additional texts for this unit could be *Listen for Rachel* (Kassem, 1986), *The Meantime* (MacKinnon, 1984), and *Maniac Magee* (Spinelli, 1990).

A Family Apart by Joan Lowery Nixon

This narrative is about a young widow, Mrs. Kelly, who gives up her six children for adoption. She sends her children out West on an orphan train so they can be adopted into new families. Frances Mary, the oldest of the children, is given the task of looking out for the youngest, Petey. Francis Mary's responsibility matures her rapidly. On their journey, she realizes why her mother gave them up. She realizes that her mother made a difficult sacrifice and really loved them. Throughout the journey,

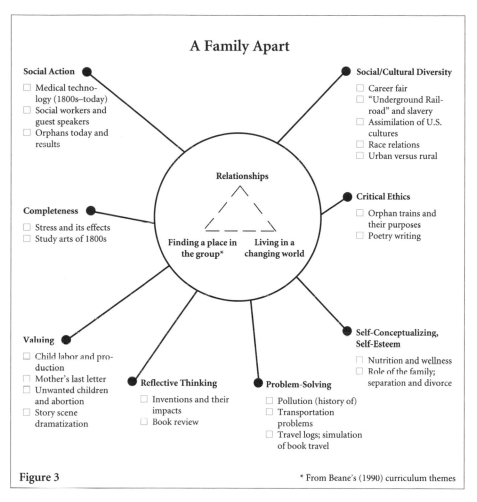

A Family Apart

Social Action
- ☐ Medical techno-
  logy (1800s–today)
- ☐ Social workers and
  guest speakers
- ☐ Orphans today and
  results

Completeness
- ☐ Stress and its effects
- ☐ Study arts of 1800s

Valuing
- ☐ Child labor and pro-
  duction
- ☐ Mother's last letter
- ☐ Unwanted children
  and abortion
- ☐ Story scene
  dramatization

Reflective Thinking
- ☐ Inventions and their
  impacts
- ☐ Book review

Problem-Solving
- ☐ Pollution (history of)
- ☐ Transportation
  problems
- ☐ Travel logs; simulation
  of book travel

Relationships

Finding a place in
the group*

Living in a
changing world

Social/Cultural Diversity
- ☐ Career fair
- ☐ "Underground Rail-
  road" and slavery
- ☐ Assimilation of U.S.
  cultures
- ☐ Race relations
- ☐ Urban versus rural

Critical Ethics
- ☐ Orphan trains and
  their purposes
- ☐ Poetry writing

**Self-Conceptualizing,
Self-Esteem**
- ☐ Nutrition and wellness
- ☐ Role of the family;
  separation and divorce

Figure 3

* From Beane's (1990) curriculum themes

the things her parents taught her help her to overcome the
many trials and tribulations.

> Themes: Family, overcoming difficulties, familial love, orphan
> experiences, separation, death, poverty, self-reliance, rejection,
> adaptive behavior, and final acceptance of reality. The central
> theme could be: Relationships. Additional texts for this unit
> could include *Wandering Girl* (Ward, 1988), *Shiloh* (Naylor,
> 1991), and *Dicey's Song* (Voigt, 1982).

Among Friends, by Caroline B. Cooney
Jennie, Hilary, and Emily, the Awesome Threesome, are best
friends. Jennie, the most dynamic of the trio, strives for perfec-
tion, which eventually destroys that relationship. Through stag-

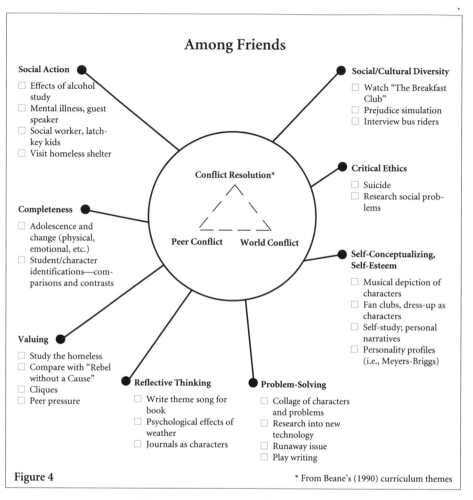

Figure 4   * From Beane's (1990) curriculum themes

gered entries of classroom journals, the story unfolds revealing the characters' fractured lives, their attempts at solutions, and their final healing and resolution.

> Themes: Friendship, materialism, abandonment, isolation, self-acceptance, self-reflection, jealousy, family relationships, and self-destruction. The central theme: Conflict resolution. Additional texts for this unit may include *The Day They Came to Arrest the Book* (Hentoff, 1982) and *False Face* (Katz, 1987).

CONCLUSION
If indeed our goals in the middle grades are to hook students on lifelong learning as well as meet the needs of the young adoles-

cent learner, we must use methods and materials conducive to these ends. Methods and materials that approach learning in an integrated and interrelated mode allows young adolescent learners the means to gather personal meaning and assimilate the information they must learn. With this in mind, an integrated literature approach to content is worthy of consideration and implementation. Not only will students gain greater insight into studied content, they will also become active, motivated learners ready to face the challenges of more complex future learning.

REFERENCES

Beane, J. A. (1990). *A middle school curriculum: From rhetoric to reality*. Columbus, OH: National Middle School Association.

Beane, J. A. (1992). Turning the floor over: Reflections on a middle school curriculum. *Middle School Journal, 23*(3), 34-40.

Brozo, W. G., & Tomlinson, C. M. (1986). Literature: The key to lively content courses, *The Reading Teacher, 40,* 288-293.

Carter, B., & Abrahamson, R. F. (1990). *Nonfication for young adults: From delight to wisdom*. Phoenix, AZ: Oryx Press.

Chall, J. (1982). *Stages of reading development*. New York: McGraw-Hill.

Cooney, C. B. (1987). *Among friends*. New York: Bantam.

Hentoff, N. (1982). *The day they came to arrest the book*. New York: Dell.

Hillerich, R. (1987). Those content areas. *Teaching K-8, 17,* 31-33.

Kassem, L. (1986). *Listen for Rachel*. New York: Avon.

Katz, W. W. (1987). *False face*. New York: Dell.

Lynch-Brown, C. (1990). Using literature across the curriculum. In J. Irvin (Ed.) *Reading and the middle school student* (p. 154-171). Boston: Allyn and Bacon.

MacKinnon, B. (1984). *The meantime*. Boston: Houghton Mifflin Company.

Mandler, J. M., & Johnson, N. S. (1977). Remembrance of things past: Story structure and recall. *Cognitive Psychology, 9,* 111-151.

Mayne, W. (1985). *Drift*. New York: Dell.

Miklowitz, G. D. (1985). *The war between the classes*. New York: Dell.

Naylor, P. R. (1991). *Shiloh*. New York: Dell.

Nixon, J. L. (1987). *A family apart.* New York: Bantam.

Norton, D. E. (1991). *Through the eyes of a child: An introduction to children's literature.* (3rd ed.). New York: Macmillan.

O'Brien, R. C. (1975). *Z for Zachariah.* New York: Macmillan.

Shanahan, T. (1969). Nine good reasons for using children's literature across the curriculum. In *Distant shores: Teacher's resource package level N* (p. 19-22). New York: McGraw-Hill.

Speare, E. J. (1958). *The witch of blackbird pond.* New York: Laurel-Leaf.

Spinelli, J. (1990). *Maniac magee.* New York: Harper Trophy.

Voigt, C. (1982). *Dicey's song.* New York: Fawcett Juniper.

Ward, G. (1988). *Wandering girl.* New York: Fawcett Juniper.

Teacher Teams: Beginning the Conversations

Good communication is as stimulating as black coffee, and just as hard to sleep after. —Anne Morrow Lindbergh

In an earlier essay in this book, "The Resurgence of Interdisciplinary Studies," Gaff refers to the *spiritual renewal* of teachers as they work with colleagues on integrated curricular designs. While teachers are reluctant at first to venture beyond their known expertise or discipline, once the math teachers are assured that they will not be expected to teach literature and vice-versa, they are ready to begin genuine conversations with other professionals. Amazingly, within a very brief time (several short meetings and interactions) they become comfortable enough and knowledgeable enough about each other's curriculum to make reference to each other's lesson content and curriculum plans.

For many years teachers have been designers of *instruction*. In fact, that design is inherent in the concept of teaching itself. Now, in addition to planning lessons, teachers are being given the license and freedom (in some cases, a mandate) to design *curriculum,* as well. Teachers have already been doing this—but behind closed doors. As someone once said, "Teaching is the second most private behavior...and you know what the first one is. Behind closed doors, no one really knows what you're teaching."

Teachers have rearranged their curriculum, adding to and deleting from the text or the curriculum guide, to make learning more meaningful. But they were "closet designers" because they thought they were not supposed to tamper with the set curriculum. However, now the doors are opening. Teachers are not only being asked to use their expertise as curriculum designers; but they are being asked to collaborate with other teachers, in other levels or departments, in an effort to combine and connect ideas that naturally go together. It is in this articulation process, this dialogue with other professionals, that the spirit is rekindled as teachers evaluate their material in synergistic ways. The power of the team prevails and the creativity that results is energizing to all involved.

Drake tells how letting go of old models was the hardest part for one team, as they "dissolved the boundaries." Drake describes several stages teachers experienced on the way to becoming a team: (1) multidisciplinary experience, (2) the interdisciplinary experience, and (3) the transdisciplinary experience. As a result of these experiences, a recommendation for team building is made for members to include as many different subjects as possible.

In another extensive study, Gehrke explores teachers' development of integrative curricula. In observing the behavior of six separate groups of teachers, the findings suggest that teachers need: time to exchange ideas about personal and professional concerns; facilitation of formal and informal activities to develop rapport and knowledge; definitions of integration to pervade the curricula they create; and to share the ideas of the original team.

Lastly, James offers an example of how teacher-planners transformed student-generated concerns about an advisement topic into a lesson plan. He demonstrates how teachers and students alike can be empowered to become curriculum designers.

How Our Team Dissolved the Boundaries

by Susan M. Drake

Teachers in Ontario who worked together on an integrated curriculum project found that their "separate" subject areas came together naturally when they worked on a theme approach to teaching.

W e were three men and three women, strangers to each other, selected from across the province to develop interdisciplinary curriculums funded by the Ontario Curriculum Superintendents' Cooperative. Each of us had expertise in a different subject area. We all had active contracts with different school boards. Our mandate was to extend the curriculum ideas in *Holistic Learning: A Teacher's Guide to Integrated Studies*[1] at the middle school level by creating a curriculum that would focus on themes.

We spent nine days together over the course of a year developing integrated curriculums. When I reviewed the journal I kept as team leader, I found that the process we had undergone was clear.

LETTING GO OF OLD MODELS
Each of us had different backgrounds in curriculum design. Some had strong leanings toward curriculums that were broken down into small, manageable parts and had a procedural base. Others were more comfortable with a more global picture that would give users an overview of the concepts involved so they could adapt them for classroom use. None had served on a committee where everyone came from such widely different backgrounds.

From *Educational Leadership*, vol. 49, no. 2, p. 20-22, 1991.
Reprinted with permission.

Our commonality was not our subject areas but rather an expressed interest in integrated curriculum. In truth, we were all in uncharted territory. As might be expected, we were divided on the question of which format to use. We spent long hours discussing hows and whys and what each of us could live with.

> **The only thing that seemed clear was that what we had once understood as curriculum design would not work for this project—we had to let go of old models.**

The only thing that seemed clear was that what we had once understood as curriculum design would not work for this project—we had to let go of old models. We came to this realization again and again. Letting go of the familiar can be a painful process, and when each of us came to a place where we couldn't find meaning, we would revert back to the way we knew best. For example, those who preferred the curriculum broken down into small, identifiable parts kept coming back to that way of structuring it. At times these regressions would seem like stumbling blocks; in hindsight we saw they were a necessary part of the process.

Each of us had to find personal meaning at every stage of the curriculum design—that was the most important thing. This could take vast amounts of time as we went over and over the same issues. As often as not, we would end up at the starting point, but not before we had wrestled enough with the concepts that they were personally meaningful.

If we had to characterize the curriculum process in one phrase, the best way to describe it would be "dissolving the boundaries." Each of us brought boundaries to this project; we saw in retrospect how artificial they were—they existed because of the ways in which we had each been taught to view the world. When we began to trust our own experience, we found that the boundaries dissolved in many different areas.

Figures 1, 2, and 3 show diagrams of multidisciplinary, interdisciplinary, and transdisciplinary approaches—visual representations of the stages we went through in the process of developing our curriculum. We were not aware of these different stages when we started, so we felt considerable relief when we identified them about midway through the process.

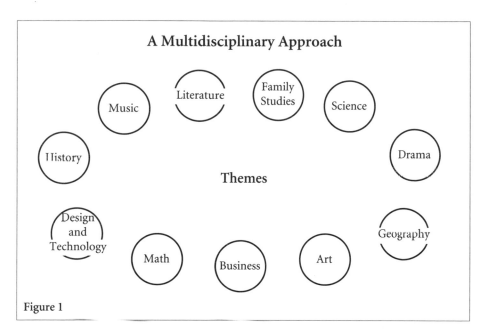

A Multidisciplinary Approach

Themes

Figure 1

THE MULTIDISCIPLINARY EXPERIENCE

As we began building our curriculum, we tried to identify the subject areas involved in each teaching activity offered so that any teacher could pick up the document and see where he or she fit in. We ourselves represented English, history, geography, science, graphic arts, intermediate special education, physical and health education, and environmental studies. As we worked on a theme, we found we could easily see the place for "our" subject area, and that it was easy to develop teaching strategies.

We eventually became able to see how some content from other areas could fit into the framework…this was our *multidisciplinary* approach.

We were able to include content from other disciplines also, but we found ourselves squeezing in such areas as mathematics that we weren't familiar with. When we involved a math teacher in the process, however, the natural place of math became obvious; we had been limited by our own narrow perspectives. So, while we began the project looking at curriculum building through the lens of our own areas of expertise, we eventually became able to see how some content from other areas could fit into the framework. Later, we realized this was our *multidisciplinary* approach.

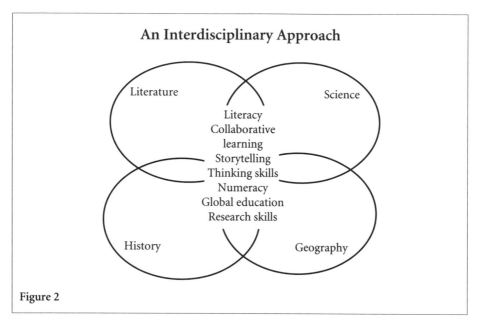

An Interdisciplinary Approach

Literature

Science

Literacy
Collaborative
learning
Storytelling
Thinking skills
Numeracy
Global education
Research skills

History

Geography

Figure 2

THE INTERDISCIPLINARY EXPERIENCE

As we became more comfortable and actually got down to sharing strategies for a theme, we found there were fewer distinctions across subjects areas than we had thought; indeed, content
overlapped. These connections existed because of the theme being explored, not because the subject areas were formally related. This discovery led us to let go of the notion that we
should teach certain facts in certain grades. We carefully labeled
each activity, breaking it down into the subject areas that were
involved. This seemed very important at the time; we wanted to
make the document user-friendly and accessible to all. That we
often had to struggle to break down an activity into different areas did not seem as important as the fact that we could do it.
We later saw this as our *interdisciplinary* stage.

THE TRANSDISCIPLINARY EXPERIENCE

After working with curriculum for several days, we began to see
the futility of breaking things down into their smallest parts.
The content and the theme were one and the same; there were
no real divisions into subject areas unless we made them. This
stage we labeled *transdisciplinary*. We abandoned the labeling of
subject areas; that is, we erased the divisions we had created up
until this point and let the activities stand by themselves. How-

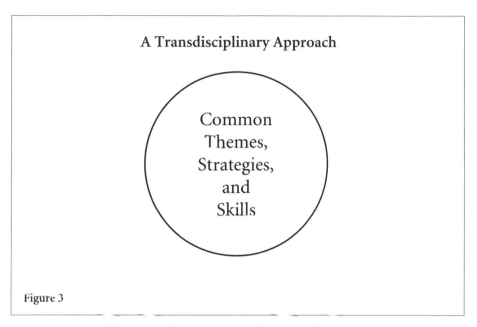

A Transdisciplinary Approach

Common Themes, Strategies, and Skills

Figure 3

ever, we did not do this until we had worked for several days on the project.

We believe that our experience is a natural progression that most people will have to go through when working on collaborative, interdisciplinary curriculum design. The more experience we had working with others of different expertise, the wider our focus became. As our lenses widened, we could see more and more of the natural connections across the curriculum. Eventually, we may become "connection experts" rather than subject experts. Each stage requires a shift in perspective, and each stage is valuable. The important objective of each stage, however, is making connections.

DROPPING OUR ASSUMPTIONS

In letting go of old models, we also had to let go of certain assumptions we had all accepted as truths. Our first concern was how to fit what we were doing with the demands of Ministry documents and school board objectives concerning skills to be acquired by certain grade levels. For example, how could we insure that the War of 1812 was properly covered in grade 8? We considered trying to take a theme and manipulate it to cover required course content, but it didn't take long to realize the impossibility of that task. We were producing this curriculum for large school boards in Ontario; there was no way we could cover mandates from individual boards and Ministry documents from across all the subject areas.

The more experience we had working with others of different expertise, the wider our focus became.

However, the real reason we could not fit content to previously determined demands was the content—we could not manipulate it to fit a linear framework of knowledge acquisition. We found that the process of generating content surrounding a theme is generic in nature. You cannot change the knowledge component of a theme simply because you are teaching it at a different grade level. We had to let go of the idea of knowledge being sequential and linear. It is not the content that will change but rather the sophistication with which one tackles the theme.

Another question that emerged was whether there was a difference between strategy and content. We found that we were often using the arts as strategies to teach facts. When did art, drama, or poetry in themselves become the focus of teaching? Again, the answer seems to be dictated by the content of the theme itself coupled with the expertise of the teacher. We found, for example, that a teacher trained in art could find ample places within any theme where specifics about art techniques had a natural place. Again, it was our limitations that put boundaries on possibilities.

A NEW APPROACH

We have decided that when subject areas are not given full acknowledgment in interdisciplinary planning, it is usually due to gaps in the curriculum team's knowledge base and experience, not the lack of proper place for the subject. For example, we recognized that music was being sadly ignored, so we brought in a music expert. When he presented us with a variety of creative ideas, we could all see the connections, but when we went back to our task, we were hard-pressed to add a rich musical dimension. This experience leads us to recommend that as many different subject areas as possible be involved in curriculum building. It may seem time consuming, but it really helps everyone to begin to see and think in terms of interconnections.

At the end of our nine days together, we looked back at what we had accomplished and were amazed at the distance we had traveled. Recently, I have talked with members of other curriculum teams involved in similar integrated studies projects. When I tell them this story, they nod their heads in agreement. They, too, are experiencing the dissolving of their individual boundaries. As we talk together and share our experiences, I believe we are beginning to accomplish our goals: We're building a base for a new approach to curriculum design.

NOTES

1. J. Miller, B. Cassie, and S. Drake, (1990), *Holistic Learning: A Teacher's Guide to Integrated Studies.* (Toronto: OISE Press).

Explorations of Teachers' Development of Integrative Curriculums

by Nathalie J. Gehrke

Integrative curriculum is like the weather: Everyone talks about it, but no one ever does anything about it—or almost no one. Education critics bemoan the fragmentation of the curriculum, but practical approaches for creating integrative curriculum are scarce.[1] In fact, rather than trying to create integrative core curriculum as in earlier eras, many curriculum developers have accepted a different meaning for the term *core*. Rather than the earlier integration of general subject areas, *core* now frequently designates a set of courses required of all students, according to Goodlad.[2] When talking to teachers, we discover that they would like to create an integrative curriculum, but their concept of one is particularly vague because most teachers have never seen or experienced an integrative curriculum; they have few, if any, images of the forms it can take.

> Most teachers have never seen or experienced an integrative curriculum; they have few, if any, images of the forms it can take.

They have no curriculum guides to turn to for exemplars. Further, they have no processes to create the curriculum and no strategies for ensuring that integrative learning experiences would result from their efforts.

By observing the behaviors of those developing integrative curriculums, and by having the developers reflect on their efforts, we can gain insights into the processes. I report here the findings from a naturalistic study of the integrative curriculum-development efforts in six separate groups of middle and high

From the *Journal of Curriculum and Supervision*, vol. 6, no. 2, p. 107-117, Winter 1991. Reprinted with permission.

school teachers working under different circumstances. The study explored what works, and how, when teachers set out to create an integrative curriculum. I hope that the findings will make future integrative curriculum-development work more manageable and therefore more likely.

PERSPECTIVES ON INTEGRATION

In several earlier eras, educators developed curriculums that they claimed were true to the concept of integration. Aikin has reported on the Eight-Year Study of the 1930s, which encouraged more than 30 high schools across the country to break from the traditional disciplines-focused curriculum.[3] The schools' found most successful on the measures of student growth and achievement had moved toward a problem- or issue-centered curriculum that allowed students to integrate knowledge from many subject areas. The Eight-Year Study saw integration as a way to get away from the fragmentation that disciplinary divisions bring.

This kind of persistent life-problems curriculum was popular in the late 1940s and early 1950s when the National Education Association advocated it as a model for educating "All American Youth."[4] Vars has described a model of integration for middle schools of the 1960s, developed further with Lounsbury.[5] Tanner and Tanner, among others, have tried to distinguish among the various forms that integrative curriculums could take.[6] They have identified correlated, fused, broadfields, core, and activity curriculum types. Helpful as these distinctions are, they do not give much guidance to teachers who want to create integrative curriculums. Although they advocate curriculum integration, the process necessary to attain it remains unexamined. This deficiency is equally true of most of the earlier writing as well; the definition of *integration* is a bit loose throughout; the authors assume that the term needs no worrying because the reader shares whatever definition used.

In 1958, Dressel proposed a more helpful definition: In the integrative curriculum, the planned learning experiences not only provide the learners with a unified view of commonly held knowledge (by learning the models, systems, and structures of the culture) but also motivate and develop learners' power to perceive new relationships and thus to create new models, systems, and structures.[7] This two-part definition began to guide my efforts to distinguish among the various ways that teachers might perceive integration and subsequently create a curriculum.

METHOD
Data Gathering and Analysis

I kept research logs and informal notes on the development processes of each of the six teacher groups over the time they were planning integrative curriculums. (I followed some groups over short terms (a day and a half) and others over longer terms (more than two years). I regularly asked the participants to reflect on the processes they used and on what was productive and unproductive. I kept notes on their comments and collected written reflections from some. I retained all lists, plans, and materials developed during the team planning sessions.

> The teams planning integrative curriculums worked under widely varying circumstances. They came with different motives.

I continually analyzed the logs, notes, and documents, comparing each new group's efforts with earlier efforts. I charted the resulting descriptions for similarities and differences. Productive strategies, obstacles, and turning points were of particular interest. The uppermost question was, of course, What works and how?

Data Source

Six teams of teachers (three high school, three middle school) took part in this study. The teams were composed of three to five members, all of whom were experienced teachers, half with fifteen or more years of service. Two teams participated in an intensive curriculum workshop that I taught and were thus composed of teachers who did not ordinarily work together. The other four teams were composed of members who, at the time of the study, were all working in a single setting, although in one case not as an ongoing team.

The teams planning integrative curriculums worked under widely varying circumstances. They came with different motives and had different amounts of time to spend and considerably different kinds of student audiences in mind as they planned. They also functioned as teams with varying levels of success. At one extreme, members of one group parted with great hostility; however, teachers in three of the continuing groups have deep, abiding friendships.

Group alpha. This group of three teachers decided three years ago that the curriculum they had been offering to their alternative school students was no longer appropriate. The three had worked together for more than ten years in a program for students who interests or personal lives did not mesh with the highly competitive high school of the district. They wanted to develop a new integrated program to replace their current individual contract system. They created their integrative curriculum over the last three years with my ongoing consultation.

> The plan was to use their own classroom as a visitation site for other teachers in the district to encourage teaming, integrative curriculum, an heterogeneous grouping.

Group beta. Four high school department chairs (English, foreign language, science, and social studies) agreed to join together to plan and carry out an integrative unit for 9th graders in their school to spark interest in integrative efforts there. They agreed, with the principal's encouragement, that if they could model this team effort, others might also be willing to try it. They met to plan the unit in a day-and-a-half retreat that they asked me to facilitate. Although they planned a unit, it was never taught because the planning efforts among the four later fell apart.

Group gamma. Three experienced middle school teachers (language arts-social studies, mathematics-science, and mathematics) had been staff development workers for two years. At their request, two were placed in a classroom setting to teach a heterogeneous 6th grade group through an integrative curriculum; the third assisted part-time. The plan was to use their own classroom as a visitation site for other teachers in the district to encourage teaming, integrative curriculum, and heterogeneous grouping. This team began developing and teaching its program during the 1987-88 school year. I have primarily acted as an observer of the group's curriculum work while playing a more active role in its inservice planning efforts.

Group delta. This group of three teachers came together in a two-and-a-half-week workshop on integrative curriculum planning. They came from different schools and so did not plan to teach the unit with each other but perhaps to use parts of it on their own. Two of the three were language arts-social studies middle school teachers. The third was a high school English teacher assigned to a middle school for the coming year. The three were not personally compatible, so the curriculum plans produced were highly fragmented. This group planning provided less in the way of insights on integrative curriculum but much about the working of teams.

Group zeta. Four high school teachers were also placed together in the integrative curriculum workshop mentioned above—two science teachers and two language arts (one English, the other speech-debate) teachers. The four worked to create two units—one based on a common concept, the other on a "great idea." These teachers also could not plan to teach the units together, so their production was mostly a learning experience. They did not have the personality conflicts of the members of the other workshop (group delta). They developed a level of trust in each other and subsequently were able to create two complete units, parts of which they also believed they could each use in their own classes.

Group eta. These five teachers all worked in a middle school teaching 6th graders. They came together in a two-day workshop to plan a unit of study they might all use individually in the months immediately following the workshop. They created a unit around the topic of Canada, one that would appear in their geography texts. At the end of the two days, they developed the unit, mapping out extensive learning activities for teachers' use, but in a follow-up session five months later only one of the teachers had begun to use the planned unit. The group blamed their lack of time to continue discussion and planning for the slow progress.

Others. These six primary groups' work formed the data base for the findings and discussion that follow. Although I have worked with other groups over the last four years, I made no attempt to systematically chart the working of those groups or to analyze the processes. These other groups have, however, had some influence on my understanding of the processes of in-

tegrative curriculum development, so I must also acknowledge
them as a data source here.

FINDINGS AND DISCUSSION

What works? Chiefly the process of planning integrative curriculums does not differ so much from other curriculum-development work as it differs in the degree of importance of certain
aspects. Further, the resulting curriculum is tied to the developers' assumptions about what constitutes integration. To direct
teachers' efforts to create integrative curriculums, we need to
give them knowledge of the importance of certain development
activities, of the various definitions of integration they can use
to create their curriculums, and time to reflect on the differences.

The Process

When this study began three years ago, I assumed that most
currently touted models of curriculum development were totally inappropriate for integrative curriculum work. (I did not
believe they were particularly useful for
traditional work either.) So with some delight I discovered the deliberative inquiry
work of Pereira, Roby, Atkins, and others—developed out of Schwab's ground-
work.[8] These processes clearly described
what the teachers I observed were doing.
They were engaged in several activities
common to deliberative inquiry: identifying the nature of the problematic situation
that prompted a new course of action,
agreeing on the goal they sought to
achieve, developing their own agenda for planning, considering
the criteria for judging the final plan (in this case, the attributes
of an integrative curriculum), generating alternatives and then
arguing about their relative merits, and finally, identifying an
acceptable plan of action.[9] They did these things not in sequential steps, but with such comprehensiveness and recursiveness
that even sequentially naming the activities does an injustice to
the process. The acknowledgment of this lack of clear sequential
activity makes the published descriptions of deliberative inquiry
cited above so useful.

> Chiefly the process of
> planning integrative
> curriculums does not
> differ so much from
> other curriculum-
> development work as
> it differs in the degree
> of importance of
> certain aspects.

Add to this deliberative process at least one feature critical to the integrative curriculum-generation process, a feature common to the work of the six groups observed: *information-exchange phases.* These phases are interspersed among the other activities but are more commonly found toward the early end of curriculum work. The purpose of these exchange periods is to share critical information, mostly about the group members. Brainstorming to create a pool of ideas is one form of exchange. But unlike the more conscious act of brainstorming, much of the exchange distributes knowledge without the participants clearly recognizing what they are doing.

I observed several different exchanges among the groups; the most obvious were among the two groups (delta and zeta) whose members had never met each other before coming together. One kind of exchange shares *knowledge of the academic* or subject-matter kind. For curriculum work to proceed, members obviously must trade this knowledge. The exchange may be as simple as finding out the others' academic majors and minors. It may move on to knowledge of sources, systems, ideas, texts, and resources: The exchange not only raises the credibility of each participant in the eyes of the others but also begins to delineate the nature of the resource pool from which the participants may draw as they seek thematic or other kinds of organizers to create learning activities.

A second kind of exchange could be called a *match of pedagogical integrators* in keeping with Shulman's pedagogical content-knowledge work.[10] Teachers hold and use pedagogical content knowledge to interpret subject matter to their students; it is teachers' specialized knowledge, but it is often an outgrowth of subject-matter knowledge structures. In the pedagogical integrator exchanges observed here, the planners checked out the themes, foci, and teaching goals the others already worked from in current classes. The checking was usually done informally, but like the beta group's exchange, it can be formal. The beta group's principal arranged interdisciplinary conversations to help the faculty seek common concepts and themes as a basis for possible later collaboration. The commonly taught concept of point of view became the organizer for the unit planned. Further exchange of information about exactly what each teacher meant by the term and how they currently taught it was part of the early planning sessions.

Another kind of knowledge exchange includes areas of *common interests* and of *individual expertise* outside the academic. Shared interests can lead a group to select themes, ideas, or concepts that are highly motivating to the teachers and therefore more likely to make the curriculum work. Individual expertise—say, in avocational areas—expands the resource pool and lends credibility to the individual. Thus, the teachers of the gamma group knew that one was a sailor, another had carpentry expertise, and the third was a sports fanatic. They could use each interest in a unit during the year. Likewise, the alpha group could use the horticulture, art, computer, and culinary interests of its members to generate themes, issues, or life situations around which units of study could be organized.

> **Shared interests can lead a group to select themes, ideas, or concepts that are highly motivating to the teachers and therefore more likely to make the curriculum work.**

The last kind of exchange observed is closely tied to the credibility issue. It is the exchange of *personal attribute information*. This information is traded, not so much in the content of the conversations, but in the process. It includes information about the participants' willingness to do their share of the work and about their carefulness, intelligence, humility, openness, and work style. Both the beta and delta groups were held together by forces beyond their choice, so when the information about personal attributes was exchanged and one or more individuals was found wanting in personal attributes or compatibility, the groups each had to discover a way to respond rather than to disband immediately. The beta group did the required planning but managed to "become too busy" later to actually have to teach the plan. The delta group also produced the required plan but subdivided it so that no one would be held accountable for work done by the others. Teams that have already been formed and required to work together have less freedom to escape each other. The problems can be endless.

Although described last here, the attribute exchange is actually the most basic of all. It functions in all group work, not just curriculum planning. As we move back through the three other kinds of exchange, our focus increasingly narrows to requisites for *curriculum* planning in groups. Exchanges of current teaching goals and themes and of academic knowledge are directly linked to curriculum planning. They are especially important to integrative curriculum planning among teachers who represent differing subject domains rather than a common domain. (Mathematics teachers have a general idea of what other mathematics teachers know, for example, but they cannot be expected to know what science teachers know except in a rather liberally educated way.)

Particularly important to integrative curriculum planning in the early stages is the exchange that makes explicit the concepts, ideas, models, and systems that the teachers hold important. Without the shared knowledge of these abstractions, the teachers' ability to create integrative curriculums at anything more than the most superficial level is impossible. That brings us to the second learning about process: the kinds of definitions people hold of *integration* and the importance of those definitions to the curriculum created.

> **Abstractions about "connectedness" and "wholeness" simply will not do.**

Definitions of Integration

As long as individuals are simply talking about integration abstractly and are not faced with creating an integrative curriculum, they can continue to hold vague definitions of *integration*. But when they actually have to create an integrative curriculum, more precision is required. Abstractions about "connectedness" and "wholeness" simply will not do. Things can be connected at many levels; wholeness can be small wholes or large ones.

The six groups studied here used a process called *curriculum webbing*.[11] At least four different definitions of *integration* emerged from the work of the six groups. The first two appear more concrete; the third and fourth, more abstract.

• *Concrete relational*—A person who holds this kind of definition of *integration* finds unity based on physical reality. Connections between or among elements are based on concurrent appearance in time, in space, or around a given object. This basic definition of *integration* is often rooted in personal experience or commonly transmitted knowledge of the world.

• *Applicative*—This definition of *integration* includes not only the concrete relationships of the first definition but also adds the idea of using or learning skills or knowledge bits, not in discrete events, but rather during other experiences where they can be used. (This application of skills and facts notion may be a distinctive teacher interpretation of *integration*.)

• *Logical*—Definitions of *integration* of this kind establish relationships through membership in a second-order (more abstract) conceptual category; through logically inferred generalizations; or through models, systems, or theoretical links.

• *Metaphoric*—Unity here is based on using attributes of one construct to shape and make sense of the relationships between elements of something else. Lakoff and Johnson have argued that a metaphoric establishment of relationships is evident even in what we might think is the most straightforward, uncolored language.[12]

The work of the eta group illustrates the concrete relational interpretation of *integration*. Their choice of a topical organizer, Canada, was the first indicator of their more physical orientation. As they began to arrange subtopics and learning activities, the definition held, as they arranged to teach everything about Canada, its people, its products, and its terrain. They decided to teach or practice certain skills through the unit, thus adding the applicative sense of integration. Their discussions did not emphasize these skills, however, and the skills are minimally evident in the written pieces the eta group produced. Little evidence exists of relationships being drawn based on abstract concepts except, perhaps, where the group used the study of government as a subtopic.

The teachers of the gamma group worked primarily from the application definition of *integration*. They chose a theme—investigations—that complemented their application definition. A recent newsletter sent to update parents on how the integrative curriculum was working described how the students used graphing and percentage-calculation skills to analyze the results of a sociological survey the students had done of their own family structures. The gamma newsletter also described how the students were using writing skills in their science work. Moreover, when explaining to me how they planned for integration, one member said: "You know how we operate. One of us says what we're doing, and the other comes up with something to go with it. We hook into what the other is doing."

They reported that an observer would hear them asking the students questions: "How does this relate to that?" (concrete relational) or "How could this apply to that?" (application). These questions could conceivably have students integrating in several of the defined ways, but the learning activities that they planned were mostly of the application sort. When I suggested having the students generalize from several learning activities (which would have embraced the logical form), they always noted the suggestion as a good point; however, I never observed any generalizing activities.

Only three of the groups—alpha, beta, and zeta—seemed to be creating logical relational curriculums. What made these three different groups—two short-term and one long-term—create logical relational curriculums? My own role as workshop instructor probably played a role in the zeta group's definition selection and use. I regularly pressed these group members to examine what they were planning against Dressel's definition. Further, I specifically guided them to develop curriculums around concepts or great ideas. The great idea they chose was, in fact, Darwin's theory of evolution. Further, I challenged them to work for activities that not only taught the theory but also helped their students seek other defensible generalizations. Logically, what you ask for seems to be what you get. Other groups, however have not shown the same inclination to respond to the press for definition as closely, especially when they are not also asked to organize around an abstract concept or great idea.

The beta group, which began its planning around the second-order concept of point of view, focused on planning a central experience to set up explorations of several generalizations about the concept. I also guided them to establish generalizations about point of view and to create substantial learning activities to teach the generalizations directly or to guide students inductively.

The alpha group's integrative concepts stem from a different configuration. They agreed two years ago to develop a curriculum with three interlocking goals: cognitive development, basic skills competence, and creativity enhancement. Although academic subject matter is important to these teachers, they do not have the constraints that many other teachers have. A long history of separation from the regular high school curriculum means they are less caught up in the specialized content of a particular department. Because their students exhibit many dysfunctional social behaviors, helping students deal with their personal lives has come before their academic progress. The constraints on their curriculum planning come not from district-required learning objectives but from student interest; if students do not like what they are studying, they simply leave or never show up. Thus, they chose theme organizers for their motivational value, but the underlying premise of most activities is getting students to develop and test out generalizations and metaphors in their academic work as well as in their personal lives.

> If students do not like what they are studying, they simply leave or never show up. Thus, [teachers] chose theme organizers for their motivational value.

Of the six groups, the alphas were the only teachers observed to encourage integrative thinking through metaphors. The highly motivating units they created used more analogical, evocative concepts, such as *roots* and *victims and villains* as organizers, rather than the equally useful but somewhat less inviting logical concepts of *cause and effect* or *justice*. Through the activities related to the themes, students were led to make poetic, not hierarchical or schematic, connections. Whether the presence of metaphoric connections was due to the need for highly motivating learning experiences or to the teachers' preferred thinking style, the use of metaphors was one of the most intriguing discoveries to come from these explorations. I am continuing to explore it with new groups of teachers. Gordon's synectics model of instruction seems particularly promising as a strategy for encouraging the use of metaphoric integrative organizers.[13]

SUMMARY AND IMPLICATIONS

Three general findings emerge from this study of the workings of six groups of teachers, each creating an integrative curriculum. First, in the act of curriculum deliberation, teachers who are creating integrative curriculums require periods of information exchange about basic personal attributes, about individually and commonly held interests and talents; about their current subject-area teaching goals, themes, and organizing concepts; and about their general academic knowledge-level expertise. Knowing that this kind of exchange must take place, the careful facilitator of integrative curriculum development will establish formal and informal activities to allow the exchange to occur early in the development work, as well as later as needed.

> We need to teach these definitions, show examples of curriculum units framed from that concept, and then guide teachers' efforts to create integrative curriculums.

A second finding relates to developing a taxonomy of definitions of *integration*. Four definitions came out of my observations of the six groups in action: concrete relational, applicative, logical, and metaphoric. The teachers' definitions of *integration* pervade the curriculum they created, especially the kinds of learning activities they described as typical.

Finally, some evidence suggests that, although some teachers already work from an abstract definition of *integration*, other teachers who do not already share that more complex definition can be taught—or perhaps *coached*—to use one, at least some of the time.

To create curriculums that will reveal multiple interrelationships to students, teachers may have more success if they hold alternative concepts of the bases of those relationships.[14] We need to teach these different definitions, show examples of curriculum units framed from that concept, and then guide teachers' efforts to create integrative curriculums based on these definitions. In time, and with continued consideration of what teachers are actually thinking and doing as they try to create integrative curriculums, we might hope to see more people doing something about integrative curriculums instead of just talking about them.

NOTES

1. Ronald S. Brandt, "On Changing Secondary Schools: A Conversation with Ted Sizer," *Educational Leadership* 45 (February 1988): 30-36; Elliot W. Eisner, "The Ecology of School Improvement," *Educational Leadership* 45 (February 1988): 24-29.

2. John I. Goodlad, "A New Look at an Old Idea," *Educational Leadership* 44 (December 1986/January 1987): 8-16.

3. Wilford M. Aikin, *The Story of the Eight-Year Study* (New York: Harper, 1942).

4. Educational Policies Commission, *Education for All American Youth* (Washington, DC: National Education Association, 1944, 1952).

5. Gordon F. Vars, ed., *Common Learnings: Core and Interdisciplinary Team Approaches* (Scranton, PA: International Textbook, 1969); John H. Lounsbury and Gordon F. Vars, *A Curriculum for the Middle School Years* (New York: Harper & Row, 1978).

6. Daniel Tanner and Laurel N. Tanner, *Curriculum Development: Theory into Practice,* 2nd ed. (New York: Macmillan, 1980), p. 480.

7. Paul L. Dressel, "The Meaning and Significance of Integration," in *The Integration of Educational Experiences*, 57th Yearbook of the National Society for the Study of Education, ed. Nelson B. Henry (Chicago: University of Chicago Press, 1958), p. 3-25.

8. Elaine Atkins, "The Deliberative Process: An Analysis from Three Perspectives," *Journal of Curriculum and Supervision* 1 (Summer 1986): 265-293; Peter Pereira, "Deliberation and the Arts of Perception," *Journal of Curriculum Studies* 16 (October-December 1984): 347-366; Thomas W. Roby, "Habits Impeding Deliberation," *Journal of Curriculum Studies* 17 (January-March 1985): 17-35; Joseph J. Schwab, *The Practical: A Language for Curriculum* (Washington, DC: National Education Association, 1970).

9. For further description, see Peter Pereira, "Deliberation and the Arts of Perception," *Journal of Curriculum Studies* 10 (October-December 1984): 347-366.

10. Lee S. Shulman, "Those Who Understand: Knowledge Growth in Teaching," *Educational Researcher* 15 (February 1986): 4-14; Lee S. Shulman, "Knowledge and Teaching: Foundations of the New Reform," *Harvard Educational Review* 57 (February 1987): 1-22.

11. Phyllis S. Levy, "Webbing: A Format for Planning Integrated Curricula," *Middle School Journal* 11 (August 1980): 26-27.

12. George Lakoff and Mark Johnson, *Metaphors We Live By* (Chicago: University of Chicago Press, 1980).

13. Bruce R. Joyce and Marsha Well, *Models of Teaching*, 3rd ed. (Englewood Cliffs, NJ: Prentice-Hall, 1986), p. 159-183.

14. Paula D. Harter and Nathalie J. Gehrke, "Integrative Curriculum: A Kaleidoscope of Alternatives," *Educational Horizons* 68 (Fall 1989): 12-17.

Refocusing Advisories, Thematically

by Michael A. James

Adventure Middle School   *Office of the Principal*
                    Memorandum
Date: *Tuesday, November 10, 1992*
From: *Ron*
To: *School Leadership Team*
Re: *Ideas gained from the NMSA Annual Conference in
          San Antonio*

*Those of us who went to the NMSA Conference have had only a
short time to process the sights and sounds of a terrific gathering of
middle school practitioners. But, we are too excited to wait! Let's
focus our next meeting on revitalizing our advisement program.
Like Jim Beane said in his 1990* Middle School Journal *article,
"Rethinking the Middle School Curriculum," we are creating a
"fragmented program without any coherent or broadly unifying
theme." (p. 2, 1990)*

By the way, there are copies (10) of Chris Stevenson's book,
Teaching Ten to Fourteen Year Olds, *in the media center. Check
it out! You might want to read chapter 10, "Advocacy and Alliance
through Advisories." I was quite struck by Stevenson's statement
on page 293 that "the irreducible essence of teacher advisory is a
commitment to kids." Isn't that what we are all about?*

See you next Wednesday at 7:30 in the conference room.

Now that's the kind of memo many more middle school
principals should send out! By coupling the creative syn-
ergy of a school's staff with some field tested planning
strategies, any advisory program—vibrant or stagnant—can be

From *Middle School Journal*, vol. 25, no. 1, p. 44-45, September 1993.
Reprinted with permission.

improved and refocused on the concerns of the kids. The rest of this article will delineate how to successfully link thematic units for learning with advisement opportunities.

Take any concerns-driven curriculum theme as suggested by Beane (1990, p. 41 & 46) and brainstorm a web or concept map of the questions middle school learners might want to find answers to given learning opportunities. One group of teachers working with these concerns decided to explore the theme of "stereotyping" (James, 1992) as they were planning an interdisciplinary unit of learning. After brainstorming guiding questions to structure the scope and sequence of the unit, the teachers were challenged to also identify advisement topics. Advisement topics are issues that emerge from the curriculum that address personal, social, emotional and/or moral/ethical concerns of students. It was a natural connection to make advisement linkages from concerns-driven curriculum that intersected personal and social concerns of youth. Many advisement topic opportunities emerged from further brainstorming by the teachers. One topic that intrigued the planners was stereotypical communications patterns—ranging from regional accents, to slang usage over the years, to the CB craze, and even gang signals and lingo.

> **It was a natural connection to make advisement linkages from concerns-driven curriculum that intersected personal and social concerns of youth.**

The teachers then asked their students to identify questions about "stereotypical communications patterns" that *they* might be interested in exploring—as part of advisement time but linked directly to the new interdisciplinary unit being planned. It may surprise the reader, but a group of 6th graders identified the following concerns/questions in a very short time.

- How does it feel to speak differently from others?
- Is it fair to kid or put-down people just because they grew up in a different region or country?
- How can we be more accepting of language differences?
- What would it be like to suddenly be a student in a non-English-speaking school?
- Do certain words and gestures mean different things to different people and of differing ages?

• Why is there so much swearing going on in the halls of our school?

By reviewing these student-generated questions, the teachers quickly realized that they—students and teachers—were creating a very exciting set of advisement topics (curriculum) that could take weeks to explore and find answers. The next step then was to organize the questions and script them into activities.

Scripting, a way of planning, takes many forms. One easily used and flexible format includes the following features:

> Unit theme:
> Advisement topics and/or questions:
> Activity outcomes or objectives:
> Possible activities:
> Assessment and/or evaluation:
> Follow-up activities:
> Related advisement topics:

What follows is but one example of how these teacher-planners turned student-generated concerns about an advisement topic into a lesson plan that lasted for a week of advisory classes (3-35 minute periods), and could easily have lasted longer:

Unit Theme: "Stereotyping"
Advisement Topics and/or Question: Stereotypical communications pattern—Do certain words and gestures mean different things to different people and of differing ages?

Activity Outcomes or Objectives: After conducting a cross-generational survey with older brothers and sisters, parents, and grandparents of non-vulgar slang and gestures, analyzing the data collected, and generating tentative conclusions, each student will re-evaluate the impact of slang and gesture usage for themselves and on others.

Possible Activities:
1. In small groups, develop a working definition of "non-vulgar slang and gestures" citing several examples of both. Pair

and share with other groups until by consensus an advisory class definition and examples emerge.

2. As a large group, develop possible survey questions to assess how people of differing ages respond to the class definition of non-vulgar slang and gestures. Develop a common survey structure to gather data.

3. Sub-divide class into four survey teams (with each student only serving on one team of choice):

    a.   those who have older brothers and/or sisters (16+ years);

    b.   those whose parents are over 30;

    c.   those who have grandparents living in town or nearby; and

    d.   those who have great-grandparents living in town or nearby.

4. Pair students within sub-groups to practice interviewing skills for gathering data using the common survey form.

5. After gathering data, compare within sub-groups who (no names) gave what examples—i.e., 17-year-old males, female parent over 30, etc., and chart results.

6. Plan a summary presentation for other sub-groups, listening to each other when not presenting.

7. As a class, discuss similarities and differences from the cross-generational survey and record these tentative conclusions to be posted for all to ponder.

Assessment and/or Evaluation: Students will write a one-page reflection paper, record a two-minute tape of reflections, and/or draw a storyboard depicting how these activities and their learnings about non-vulgar slang and gestures impact themselves and others.

Follow-up Activities:

1. Write and produce a skit or short play that captures the spirit of the survey data.

2. Read selected young adolescent novels for ideas about how fictional characters used slang and gestures.

3. Survey other sixth graders about non-vulgar slang and gestures to broaden the data base.

4. Watch TV sitcom programs in which children their age

are characters and note their use of slang and gestures and the impact it has on the adult characters.

5. Keep a log of slang and gestures you hear and see in the mall, at a school social event, at church or other family-oriented functions.

Related Advisement Topics:

1. How do slang phrases and gestures vary among and between various racial and/or ethnic groups?

2. How are slang and CB talk similar? Different?

3. How accurate (and fair) is stereotyping a person by what or how they say or do something?

By integrating student-generated concerns/questions into advisement topics and activities which directly parallel the focus of an interdisciplinary unit in progress, teachers are actualizing Stevenson's "irreducible essence of...advisory." Furthermore, because both teachers and students are empowered to become curriculum developers of significantly interesting, engaging, and integrative opportunities that stress the use of skills and knowledge to produce deeper and richer insights into the world of youth and others, these processes also satisfy Beane's hope that "...advisory, and other 'specials' might more appropriately be integrated into ongoing units" (p. 4).

REFERENCES

Beane, J. A. (1990). "Rethinking the middle school curriculum." *Middle School Journal, 21*(1-5).

Beane, J. A. (1990). *A middle school curriculum: From rhetoric to reality.* Columbus, OH: National Middle School Association.

James, M. A. (Spring 1992). "Shibboleths of reform." *Current Issues in Middle Level Education, 1*(1).

Stevenson, C. (1992). *Teaching ten to fourteen year olds.* New York, NY: Longman.

The Final Analysis: Two Views

I want to talk about learning. But not the lifeless, sterile, futile, quickly forgotten stuff that is crammed into the mind of the poor helpless individual tied into his seat by ironclad bonds of conformity! I am talking about LEARNING—*that insatiable curiosity that drives the adolescent boy to absorb everything he can see or hear or read about gasoline engines in order to improve the efficiency and speed of his "cruiser."* ...—Carl Rogers, *Freedom to Learn for the '80s,* 1983, p. 18.

To end this collection with two very different critiques of integrated learning seems appropriate. For one to embrace an idea while another rejects that same idea is inherent in the human experience.

Many may approach this book with a built-in bias. Some who are already enchanted with the idea of integrating their curricula are looking for ideas, clarification, models, and confirmation of their own thinking on the matter. These educators are looking for creative ways to teach and inventive ways for children to learn. Others, who are less inclined toward radical change, proceed more cautiously. Just as the paradox of the half-full, half-empty glass suggests, curriculum integration is perhaps best viewed from both perspectives. In the differing critiques, one is led toward more balanced judgments.

"Just because an activity crosses subject-matter lines does not make it worthwhile" is the plea heralded by Brophy and Alleman in a succinct but worthy piece that cautions against looking at curriculum integration as a panacea for educational reform. The authors offer five considerations that include examining the educational value, time, distortion of content, ill-conceived integration ideas, and the sometimes unpreparedness of students to complete the prescribed activities. While the authors do not condemn curriculum integration, they caution that certain criteria should be applied when planning for it.

From another perspective, students' perceptions of an integrated unit are set forth in a case study. Mansfield's findings seem somewhat positive in light of current educational concerns. Students felt they had more freedom and choice, the level of student commitment was high, positive interactions and cooperative behaviors were promoted, and students indicated an awareness of the traditionally fragmented vs. the more holistic learning process with integrated units. The article ends with suggestions to move toward integrated learning models.

While there are numerous and divergent views of curriculum integration, the most useful analysis—the final analysis of course—is developed personally through individual assessment and critique of the process, and the results.

A Caveat: Curriculum Integration Isn't Always a Good Idea

by Jere Brophy & Janet Alleman

Just because an activity crosses subject-matter lines does not make it worthwhile; it must also help accomplish important educational goals.

Curriculum integration is sometimes necessary to teach about topics that cut across or transcend school subjects. Even when integration is not necessary, it is often desirable, as when content drawn from one subject is used to enrich the teaching of another (period artwork used in history) or when skills learned in one subject are used to process or apply information learned in another (debates or report writing in social studies). However, curriculum integration is not an end in itself but a means for accomplishing basic educational goals. Furthermore, recommended activities may not help achieve those goals, nor are they always implemented effectively.

We offer this caveat because, in the course of examining recent elementary social studies series, we saw many suggestions made in the name of integration that we consider counterproductive. Too often, activities described as ways to integrate social studies with other subjects either lack educational value in any subject or promote progress toward significant goals in another subject but not in social studies.

Many of these activities are pointless busywork (alphabetizing the state capitals). Others may have value as language arts activities but don't belong in social studies curriculum (exercises that use social studies content but focus on pluralizing nouns).

From *Educational Leadership*, vol. 49, no. 2, p. 66, 1991.
Reprinted with permission.

Moreover, many suggested activities require time-consuming artistic or construction work. Some of these develop—or at least allow for—opportunities to use social studies knowledge (constructing maps of the school), but others simply lack educational value (carving pumpkins to look like U.S. presidents). The same is true of various role-play, simulation, collage, and scrapbook activities.

So-called integration activities sometimes even distort social studies content. For example, a unit on pioneer life includes a sequencing-skills exercise built around five steps in building log cabins. Three of these five steps are arbitrarily imposed rather than logically necessary. The authors apparently included this exercise not because it developed key knowledge about pioneer life, but because they wanted to put an exercise in sequential ordering somewhere in the curriculum.

Ill-conceived integration ideas also sometimes require students to do things that are strange, difficult, or even impossible. One activity calls for students to use pantomime to communicate one of the six reasons for the Constitution as stated in its preamble. We do not think that social studies time should be spent practicing pantomime skills, but even if we did, we would select a more appropriate subject for pantomime than reasons for the Constitution.

> An activity is appropriate because it promotes progress toward significant educational goals, not merely because it cuts across subject-matter lines.

Finally, suggested activities sometimes call for students to do things they are not prepared to do, either because the task is ambiguous (drawing a hungry face) or because it requires them to use knowledge that has not been taught in the curriculum and is not likely to have been acquired elsewhere (having 1st graders role-play scenes from Mexico when all they have learned about Mexico is its location on the map).

In view of these problems, educators should consider integration a potential tool that is feasible and desirable in some situations but not in all. An activity is appropriate because it promotes progress toward significant educational goals, not merely because it cuts across subject-matter lines. Furthermore, in assessing the time spent in integrated activities versus subject-area ones, educators should weigh the cost-effectiveness of the activities in accomplishing each subject's major goals.

Before we have students engage in activities designed to promote curriculum integration, let's apply criteria:

1. Activities should be educationally significant, ones desirable even if they did not include the integration feature.

2. Activities should foster, rather than disrupt or nullify, accomplishment of major goals in each subject area.

Author's note: This work is sponsored in part by the Institute for Research on Teaching, College of Education, Michigan State University. The institute is funded from a variety of federal, state, and private sources, including the U.S. Department of Education and Michigan State University. The opinions expressed here do not necessarily reflect the position, policy, or endorsement of the funding agencies.

Students' Perceptions of an Integrated Unit: A Case Study

by Barbara Mansfield

ocial studies is a subject area that can act as a vehicle for presenting the skills and concepts that permeate the whole curriculum (Charlesworth and Miller 1985). Within the primary division (K-3), the program is frequently presented in this fashion, using social studies as an umbrella under which a variety of subject perspectives and skills can be brought to bear on a specific topic or theme. At the junior level (4-6), this integrated approach is rarely used because teachers tend to present a subject-based program. A provincial review conducted by the Ontario Ministry of Education (1985) reported that of the forty-two schools reviewed, only a "few" (1-25%) junior-level classrooms were consistently integrated. In this case, an integrated curriculum was defined as "learning which is synthesized across traditional subject lines, and learning experiences which are arranged in order to be mutually reinforcing."

> The term *integrated studies* is interpreted in several ways and is applied to practice in varying degrees.

While critics of the thematic way of organizing social studies programs have said that this approach lacks vigor and continuity, theme-based units can have a number of strengths. They may be relevant to the students' interests and experiences, have the capacity to deal with emerging issues, and ensure that specific topics are covered (Wood 1987). They also present a framework upon which the integrated approach can be developed.

From *Social Studies*, vol. 80, no. 4, p. 135-140, July-August 1989.
Reprinted with permission.

The term *integrated studies* is interpreted in several ways and is applied to practice in varying degrees. Integration occurs when the boundaries between the content of various subjects are weak or blurred. In other words, the content of each subject is subordinate to some idea that reduces its isolation from the others (Bernstein 1975). The curriculum involved may be teacher developed and controlled or predominantly child initiated. If it is the latter, many topics may be dealt with at the same time within a classroom because each child may be working in his or her own area of interest. When the theme is teacher developed, it tends to take the form of a unit of work that cuts across the traditional subject lines. The manner in which learning is encouraged can range from formal class lessons to group activities to independent research.

Integration also occurs along a continuum from a partial to a total inclusion of the program subjects (UNESCO 1982), and many teachers integrate only part of their program. For instance, they may cut across the disciplines of language arts, social studies, and science to present a theme about "The Community." Those subject areas that are not included within the theme are dealt with in the usual manner. In some schools, integrated studies involve not only the cooperative use of the various disciplines' skills and information but also cooperation among teachers to develop and present the different aspects of the theme in a coherent and meaningful way (Schools Council Integrated Studies 1972).

Although several studies have examined and described the organizational factors and the processes involved within particular integrated approaches to organizing curriculum (UNESCO 1982; Ladenberg and Silfern 1983; Boehnlein and Ritty 1977; Cameron 1986), little has been said about how children perceive these practices. Do nine- to twelve-year-olds understand the implications of integrated studies as compared with the traditional subject-oriented program? Have they a preference for one over the other, and if so, why?

The descriptive case study presented in this article examines how a class of grade 5/6 students reacted to, and what ideas the students had about, an integrated unit in which they participated. It looks at the way in which the children associated many of the process changes with integrated studies.

METHODOLOGY

Participant observation and open-ended interviews with the students and the teacher were the two principal forms of data collection. During the five-week period in which the integrated unit was in progress, I spent three days a week observing in the classroom. Both individual and small-group interviews were conducted with seventy-five percent of the students whose names have been changed. This involved all students for whom I had parental permission to interview formally. I used a constant comparative methodology (Glasser and Strauss 1967; Glasser 1978) to analyze the collected data and record emergent categories.

The Setting

Maple Hill School, located in a middle-class suburban area of a small Ontario city, is a pleasant modern building housing approximately 350 kindergarten to grade 6 students. Teaching methods and program approaches vary with the teachers, but the tendency has been for classes to be more activity oriented in the primary grades (K-3) while the junior division (4-6) presents a subject-oriented and more traditional program.

> The teacher used social studies as "the glue that bonds together the elements of the curriculum for young children."

The grade 5/6 class that is the focus of this study was composed of seventeen grade 5 and ten grade 6 students. In addition to their classroom teacher, Mrs. Ball, there were also specialists responsible for teaching music, French, and physical education. The manner in which program responsibilities were broken down promoted a very fragmented approach to curriculum.

The Integrated Unit

Mrs. Ball decided to use the social studies theme of "Life in Egypt" as the basis for developing a five-week integrated unit with her class. Almost all the time spent in the regular classroom was devoted to activities surrounding the theme. In this way, the teacher used social studies as "the glue that bonds together the elements of the curriculum for young children" (Broman 1982, 203).

The unit was teacher developed and controlled to a great extent. Three strands made up its framework.

(a) Activity cards for which students had both compulsory and choice selections were developed by the teacher. These cards were divided into categories such as information, creative writing, word study, research, art, and problems.

> The children tended to view the integrated unit in two ways. Some equated doing activity cards with integration while others suggested that integration involved focusing upon a topic and learning a lot about that topic.

(b) Teacher-initiated formal lessons were taught and followed by activities that supported the lesson focus.

(c) Other activities, which included creating a large mural, seeing films and slides, preparing for Egyptian Day, writing in journals, reading stories, and working on child-initiated projects were also part of the program.

The students were given notebooks in which they were to keep notes, pictures, and any written work that their activities involved. Tracking sheets were pasted on the front and back covers of the notebooks. These sheets listed all of the activity card titles with the compulsories underlined. Columns entitled "date completed" and "comments" were filled in by the teacher as the students completed each activity. When the unit was finished, the students had a complete record of what they had accomplished.

Mrs. Ball worried about the lack of math included in the unit's activities so she took time out during the first few weeks to teach formal math lessons. As time passed, the class got more deeply involved in the Egyptian theme, and Mrs. Ball resigned herself to giving up the lessons until the end of the unit.

STUDENTS' PERCEPTIONS

As the student interviews progressed, two points became evident. The children tended to view the integrated unit in two ways. Some equated doing activity cards with integration while others suggested that integration involved focusing upon a topic and learning a lot about that topic. In some cases, students combined both views.

During the unit, many procedural changes did take place, which influenced the classroom interactions. Although students valued these changes and attributed them to the integrated approach, many of them were not necessarily inherent to this particular approach. Approaches that give students the opportunity to make choices, promote informal communication within the class, and use an activity-based approach to learning are common to several programming styles. But it is important to note that most of the students had definite opinions to express about what they thought integrated studies involved and how this approach differed from the more subject-based one they normally experienced.

The Tension Between Autonomy and Control

Children felt that they had much more freedom and choice during this unit than they had within the regular program. Much of this feeling was derived from the activity-card portion of the unit when the students were allowed to choose their own activities. They had few time limitations placed upon them and were given more freedom to interact with other students. At the same time, the children clearly realized that this freedom was limited. They knew that the teacher retained control of the program, but they accepted this without question because the limited freedom of choice was much more than they usually had. Andy and Charlie's conversation exemplifies this understanding.

A: Well, like you can choose any topic at all and like, sometimes the teacher just says, "You do this and you do that." But you can choose what you want to do.

B: [B is the interviewer] So choice has a lot to do with it?

C: Yeah.

C: Because you have freedom. She tells you what to do, and this time she can tell you what to do but there's more things to do. Like, she tells you to do cards, and there's so many different topics with the cards. Not just one thing to do.

Another more subtle control on the children's behavior was the culminating activity, "Egyptian Day." The students knew that on the final day of the unit they would be making several presentations to their parents and other students within the school. Mrs. Ball introduced potential plans for Egyptian Day on the first day of the unit, saying: "Before we get to Egyptian Day, you're going to have to work hard learning things about Egypt." The importance of this celebration and its influence on the children is evident from the following remarks:

H: And then they [the students] think, well, if there is the Egyptian Day at the end, we'll work hard because I might get the part I want.

K: And everything is going to be hanging up on the walls.

H: And if they do good on one part, like they wrote funny poems and they might be the jester—not the jester but the person who announces it.

I: Well, people are trying hard for things to be neat because people are going to be coming and looking in their notebooks and looking at their art work and what they've done.

Commitment

During the five weeks of the unit, the level of student commitment to the activities involved was high. Indicators of this commitment included positive changes in behavior, pride in work, completion of tasks, high level of interest, and perception of time.

Several individuals discussed how their behavior, as well as that of their fellow students, had changed and the reasons responsible for those changes. They believed that the students were more involved in their work and much happier in class. The major reason for this change was a lessening of teacher talk and teacher direction, which allowed for more student choice and active participation in classroom activities. This lessened the chance of being bored and thus getting into trouble. Connie presented this point of view when she stated:

The belief that this unit was more fun than the normal program appears to have strongly influenced the children's attitudes and behavior.

Yeah, kids don't seem to be goofing off as much. They don't seem to be yelling out and that's because the teacher isn't talking too much. So they're really doing basically their own things. As I said, the teacher's not really telling them what activity they should be doing. I think they goof off a lot because they wanted to do their own thing really. So the teacher really just tells you what part of the unit you're going to be doing today.

The belief that this unit was more fun than the normal program appears to have strongly influenced the children's attitudes and behavior. Was the work fun because it was easier (as some believed) or was it easier because it was fun? In either case, activities that are enjoyable tend to gain our interest and commitment. Also, because the students took on ownership of their activities, they worked harder to complete them properly.

It is interesting to note that Mrs. Ball's opinions on behavior during the unit were very similar to those of her students.

> They're actually working. . . . [During the usual program George and Ronnie] would just sit there. They'd be quiet, or they'd try to get somebody's attention in the room, or they'd throw an eraser to get somebody. Like, they weren't really keen on what they were doing. . . . They've been working just fine. You know, [Bill's] the only one that really at times has still goofed off a bit, but that's only been after he's usually worked for a good half-hour block, which is far more than he worked before. . . . [Y]esterday afternoon, you could have heard a pin drop in there, and they were all so enthused about making their names in hieroglyphics and hanging them over their own heads.

The students appeared to be very proud of their work. Several children indicated pride in the art and research work.

The students appeared to be very proud of their work. Several children indicated pride in the art and research work. Also, having a special notebook just for the unit was a strong factor in the promotion of this pride. Edith and Emily stated outright that they were proud of their notebooks, whereas Sally liked hers because she felt that it would hold good memories for her of what she had done during the unit. The students also felt good about the positive comments that the teacher had written on their tracking pages. Marty and Alice presented another reason for liking their special notebooks:

M: Well, I like mine. I think it's neat too. . . . You get your own book to have it all in instead of looking all over all these books, one for art and one for math and everything.

A: It's neat; it teaches a topic. You just don't scribble it or something. You just make it neat. . . ., [as if] it's one of your best notebooks.

There was a concerted effort on the part of the majority of students from the start of the unit to complete their assigned activities. Students frequently worked on these tasks when there was no pressure to do so. The following excerpt from my field notes presents an example of this phenomenon.

> I arrived just before recess was over. It was raining, so students had stayed in. Many of them had already started working on a card, and Mrs. Ball was busy discussing things with individual students.

Why did the children put in so much extra time and effort on their activities? Emily suggested, "Just to get them finished, and we enjoy doing them, I guess."

Completing activity cards became a strong personal and social goal in the class. Children were often overheard comparing the number of cards they had finished. In one case, Susan spent five minutes drifting from one person to the next, asking how many cards each had done. Amy completed thirty-nine out of a possible forty-two activities and became the class heroine for this feat. Her classmates kept a close watch on her progress throughout the unit. The one major exception to this race was Cornelius, who, by the end of the unit, had completed few of his obligatory assignments. He seemed to have trouble finding information and was easily distracted from his tasks. Much of his time was spent in watching others complete their work.

The level of interest remained high throughout the unit. The variety of activities available appeared to promote this feeling. When asked why she thought that activities were interesting or fun, Sylvia replied,

S: Well, usually the work, it gets long and boring. You have to do so much written work. I like art a lot, and so you get to do art and stuff, play games, and learn a lot from these things too. And the research cards are lots of fun 'cause most of them are easy and they're neat to find out facts about.

The content of the unit was also innately interesting to the children. When I asked the students to write down their favorite thing about the unit, a third of them focused upon the information they had learned rather than the processes in which they had been involved. These students said that they liked things such as King Tut, pyramids, mummification, gods and goddesses.

The high level of interest prompted the children to discuss the unit at home with their parents. Several students brought things from home to share with the class—for example, hieroglyphic charts, Egyptian photographs, pictures, and money. Helen brought in a wooden model of a pyramid, which she and her father had constructed at home.

The old saying of "Time passes quickly when you're having fun" seems to have been borne out here. The following comment, which Heather made about wasting time, exemplifies the level of commitment that many students had toward their work.

H: It wastes time too.

B: How does it waste time?

H: Well, you think while you're writing you've been there for half an hour, but actually it's been about an hour that you've been working on one [activity].

B: Why do you think that happens?

H: Because you work on it so hard and then you don't know how fast the time went by.

Interaction

One of the goals most teachers have is to promote positive interaction and helping behaviors among their students. The Egyptian unit's structure appeared to encourage this. Children were allowed to "visit" with each other freely, and frequently they helped one another to find needed resources or information. In many situations, they shared ideas and reacted to each other's completed work. At times, they shared the same activity, working either in a parallel fashion or together.

When the children chatted with others, the majority of their talk focused upon the Egyptian theme, with both content and process being discussed. Among the several reasons that students went visiting were: looking for new ideas, getting information on a specific topic or about the way in which to do an activity, trying to locate a card or resource material, being curious about what others had done, and discussing social items that had little to do with school work. The following excerpt from a group interview indicates that the students were aware of the different reasons for visiting.

B: I've noticed that while they're doing their work, some people get up and wander around and visit for a while. Do you know what sorts of things these children tend to talk about?

K: Well, some people want to know questions.

S: And some just want to read their things.

H: I like going around because if I can't think of anything then I just go around and look at what the other people are doing to get some ideas.

S: You ask some people when you need to know something, like something on Anubis and somebody was doing an activity card on Anubis. You could just ask them.

The classroom environment became a very supportive one during the progress of the unit. The helping behaviors observed were spontaneous in nature, arising from the natural interaction among the children rather than being superimposed by a formal group structure that the teacher controlled. This type of behavior was quite evident during a class assignment in which each child took on the persona of an ancient Egyptian god, goddess, or pharaoh. In preparation for doing this, each student had to research his or her character. Throughout the initial period of time allotted to this task, there were many incidents of students' finding and sharing information about each other's characters. This activity engendered an excitement about and interest in helping others to locate needed information. The children identified strongly with their chosen characters. This response was very similar to that which McCarthy and Braffman (1985) reported when they observed children in the process of assuming Victorian identities as part of a history project.

The children suggested that interaction patterns with the teacher had changed too. Hilda's comment that "she [the teacher] can wander as much as she wants now instead of hav-

> The classroom environment became a very supportive one during the progress of the unit.

ing to stay by the board when she has to teach a lesson" suggests that this approach to teaching-learning might promote greater teacher-student interaction. Several comments made by the students support this view. These students also felt that the integrated approach was more difficult for the teacher because she now had to deal with the many topics dictated by the activity cards. They felt it must be hard for the teacher continually to change focus as she moved around the room to help different students with a variety of topics.

Fragmentation/Continuity of the Program

During their interviews, the students were asked whether or not they saw a difference between the unit and their ordinary school program. The answers given by some students indicate their awareness of how fragmented the regular program was and how the integrated approach promoted a more holistic learning process.

K: Well, I like doing subjects and that, but I like doing Egypt. It's really interesting, and I think I like working on a topic better because it's more . . . one topic, you don't have to switch from one subject to the next. Otherwise, the next day you carry on from the last subject, and you've done so many after that or if it's at the end of the day, you've done so many like the next day you just forget. Like, I like doing the integrated unit 'cause you don't have to change.

C: I thought it was kind of better because, well, usually you keep changing subjects, and this time you just centered yourself on usually one thing, and you can do that all day or keep going.

Mrs. Ball's comments on this topic tended to support the idea presented by the children. At one point, she discussed her science program. In her opinion, because of the lack of time and the spacing between lessons, the carry-over was not good and the program had no clear focus. When comparing this view with her feelings about the components of the regular program, Mrs. Ball saw many positive aspects in the integrated unit. She compared her sense of direction in the Egyptian unit to what happened during a science unit, which she had taught at an earlier date:

We didn't do anything, I just felt like, well, the whole month had gone by and we had one note in our notebook. There was nothing to mark. There was nothing to evaluate. I don't think the kids particularly got a lot out of it. I didn't feel like I got a lot out of it. This way there is a sense of knowing where you're going and what you're doing, and you're immersed in it.

EVALUATION OF THE INTEGRATED UNIT

By changing the mode of program organization and presentation, the teacher affected a multitude of classroom behaviors. The way in which she interacted with the children within pedagogical situations became more individualized and less formal. Students were permitted to socialize with each other more frequently, which, in turn, often led to peer teaching situations. Evaluation became an ongoing, integral part of the program rather than the final step. Finally, children and teacher began to view subject content as being somewhat overlapping rather than being molecular or separate in nature. As mentioned earlier, all of these elements are not necessarily the outcomes of an integrated program, but they were significant changes in the minds of both the students and the teacher.

> Evaluation became an ongoing, integral part of the program rather than the final step.

Participating in the integrated unit was a positive experience for all the students who were interviewed. Throughout the duration of the unit, a highly supportive environment was created, one in which individuals had more autonomy in choosing their activities and how they went about completing them. They also were able to socialize with others in a variety of ways not usually permitted within the normal program.

The fact that each student was working on his or her own activity much of the time may have contributed to this positive attitude in another way. The constant comparison that students make about each other's progress and level of competency when completing either group or class tasks was missing in this situation. (Although the students often talked about their work to each other, they were usually involved with different activities, so the discussion was descriptive or helping in tone rather than comparative.) Therefore, individuals could work at their own speed and level of ability without the pressure of being judged constantly against their peers. This also encouraged the teacher to look at each child's work within that child's own framework of ability.

The high level of student commitment to the unit's activities appears to have been promoted by several factors. The first has already been discussed—autonomy. The holistic approach to studying a topic was a second significant factor. Both the students and the teacher enjoyed the lack of fragmentation within the Egyptian unit. Both felt that not having to change their focus from subject to subject was a relief and allowed them to learn in more depth and scope.

Finally, the children's commitment was secured by the variety of processes in which they were involved and the fact that much of the topic's information was innately interesting. Several students discussed how much they liked being able to paint, build models, write poetry and stories, and watch films rather than always having to make notes in their notebooks as they usually did during regular classes. They also found the Egyptian topics fascinating and were often encouraged to read further to find out more information about a specific topic.

> Individuals could work at their own speed and level of ability without the pressure of being judged constantly against their peers.

Teachers who are interested in attempting the integrated studies approach for the first time might consider (a) potential student interest in the theme, (b) a variety of activity processes, (c) some degree of student autonomy to be built into the unit, and (d) ways in which social interaction could be encouraged. This study describes a program that was only partially integrated, because a few subjects were held separate. For the teacher who is a novice in this area, this approach may be a first step on the path toward complete integration.

REFERENCES

Bernstein, B. 1975. *Class, codes and control* (Vol. 3). London: Routledge and Kegan Paul.

Boehnlein, M., and J. Ritty. 1977. Integration of the communication arts curriculum: A review. *Language Arts* 54(4): 372-77.

Broman, B. 1982. *The early years in childhood education.* Chicago: Rand McNally.

Cameron, B. 1986. You are there: Reading, feeling, thinking history. North Dakota University, Grand Forks: (ERIC Document #ED278590).

Charlesworth, R., and N. Miller. 1985. Social studies and basic skills in the early childhood classroom. *The Social Studies* 76(1): 34-37.

Glaser, B. 1978. *Theoretical sensitivity.* Mill Valley, CA: Sociology Press.

Glaser, B., and A. Strauss. 1967. *The discovery of grounded theory.* Chicago: Aldine Publishing Company.

Ladenberg, V., and M. Silfern. 1983. A year as woodland Indians: The social studies core of the third grade. *Moral Educational Forum* 8(2): 24-30.

McCarthy, L., and E. Braffman. 1985. Creating Victorian Philadelphia: Children reading and writing the world. *Curriculum Inquiry* 15(2): 121-51.

Ontario Ministry of Education. 1985. *Education in the junior division: A look at forty-two schools.* (Provincial: Review Report No. 5).

Schools Council Integrated Studies. 1972. *Exploration man: An introduction to integrated studies.* Oxford: Oxford University Press.

United Nations Educational, Scientific, Cultural Organization. 1981. *Integrating subject areas in primary education.* Bangkok, Thailand: (ERIC Document Reproduction Service No. ED 238 536).

Wood, F. 1987. *The social education framework: P-10.* Ministry of Education, Schools' Division, Victoria, Australia.

Authors

Janet Alleman is Professor, Department of Teacher Education, Michigan State University, College of Education, Erickson Hall, East Lansing, MI 48824-1034.

James A. Beane teaches at National-Louis University, Madison, Wisconsin.

Jere Brophy is Co-Director of the Institute for Research on Teaching and Distinguished Professor, Department of Teacher Education, Michigan State University, College of Education, Erickson Hall, East Lansing, MI 48824-1034.

Allyne Brumbaugh teaches second grade at Greenacres Elementary School in Scarsdale, New York.

Renate Nummela Caine is Associate Professor and Executive Director of the Center for Research in Integrative Learning/Teaching, California State University, School of Education, 5500 University Parkway, San Bernardino, CA 92407.

Geoffrey Caine is a consultant and an adjunct faculty member. The University of the Redlands, Whitehead Center for Lifelong Learning, 2630 Cincinnati St., San Bernardino, CA 92407.

Richard J. Cummings is Director of the Honors Program, Professor of Languages and Literature, and Adjunct Professor of Theatre at the University of Utah. He is also Chair of the Fellowship Committee of Phi Kappa Phi.

Susan M. Drake is an Associate Professor, Faculty of Education, Brock University, St. Catherines, Ontario, Canada L2R 3A1.

Robin Fogarty is Creative Director at IRI/Skylight Publishing, Inc., 200 E. Wood St., Suite 274, Palatine, IL 60067.

Andrea Foster teaches sixth-grade science at Sul Ross Middle School in San Antonio, Texas.

Jerry G. Gaff is Vice President for Planning at Hamline University. He is the author of *General Education Today* (San Francisco: Jossey-Bass, 1983) and is co-author of *A New Vitality in General Education* (Washington, D.C.: Association of American Colleges, 1988).

Nathalie J. Gehrke is Professor, College of Education, University of Washington, Seattle, WA 98195.

Heidi Hayes Jacobs is Adjunct Associate Professor in the Department of Curriculum and Teaching at Columbia University in New York. She consults with schools and districts nationally on curriculum reform, school restructuring, and instructional thinking skills strategies. She is the editor of *Interdisciplinary Curriculum: Design and Implementation* (ASCD, 1990).

Michael A. James teaches at Wichita State University, Wichita, Kansas.

Holly Johnson teaches at South Oldham Middle School, Crestwood, Kentucky.

Richard Kimpston is Professor Emeritus at the University of Minnesota.

Rosemary F. Kolde is Executive Vice President, Great Oaks Institute of Technology and Career Development, Cincinnatti, Ohio.

Shayne Konar, currently [1991] on parental leave, teaches in Grand Forks, British Columbia.

Anne C. Lewis, formerly executive editor of *Education USA*, is a freelance writer living in the Washington, D.C. area.

Barbara Mansfield is a member of the Faculty of Education at Queen's University in Kingston, Ontario, Canada.

Joan Maute has been a team coordinator and lead teacher. She currently [1989] is a teacher at Hill Middle School and social studies coordinator for Indian Prairie District #204 in Naperville, Illinois.

Betty Jean Eklund Shoemaker is a Curriculum Coordinator for the Eugene (Ore.) Public Schools. She was the facilitator for the task force that developed the *Education 2000 Integrated Curriculum*. She is currently [1991] completing a doctorate in curriculum and instruction at the University of Oregon, Eugene.

Anju Relan is Professor Emeritus at the University of Minnesota.

J. Lea Smith teaches at the University of Louisville, Kentucky.

Tupper Webster is Coordinator, Early Childhood Education Program, University of Maryland—Baltimore County, Baltimore.

Gordon F. Vars is Professor of Education Emeritus at Kent State University, Kent, Ohio.

Acknowledgments

Grateful acknowledgment is made to the following authors and agents for their permission to reprint copyrighted materials.

Phi Delta Kappan for "Integrated Learning for a Competitive Work Force" by Rosemary F. Kolde. From *Phi Delta Kappan* vol. 72, no. 6, p. 453-455, February 1991. Reprinted with permission of *Phi Delta Kappan*. Copyright © 1991 by *Phi Delta Kappan*. All rights reserved.

The Association for Supervision and Curriculum Development for "Understanding a Brain-Based Approach to Learning and Teaching" by Renate Nummela Caine and Geoffrey Caine. From *Educational Leadership* vol. 48, no. 2, p. 66-70, 1990. Reprinted with permission of the Association for Supervision and Curriculum Development. Copyright ©1990 by ASCD. All rights reserved.

National Forum: The Phi Kappa Phi Journal for "The Interdisciplinary Challenge: Connection and Balance" by Richard J. Cummings. Reprinted from *National Forum: The Phi Kappa Phi Journal* Volume LXIX, Number 2, Spring 1989. Copyright © by Richard J. Cummings. By permission of the publishers. All rights reserved.

Anju Relan and Richard Kimpston for "Curriculum Integration: A Critical Analysis of Practical and Conceptual Issues." Paper presented at the annual meeting of the American Educational Research Association, Chicago, IL, April 1991. All rights reserved.

Phi Delta Kappan for "Getting Unstuck: Curriculum as a Tool of Reform" by Anne C. Lewis. From *Phi Delta Kappan* vol. 71, no. 7, p. 534-538, March 1990. Reprinted with permission of *Phi Delta Kappan*. Copyright © 1990 by *Phi Delta Kappan*. All rights reserved.

National Forum: The Phi Kappa Phi Journal for "The Resurgence of Interdisciplinary Studies" by Jerry G. Gaff. Reprinted from *National Forum: The Phi Kappa Phi Journal* Volume LXIX, Number 2, Spring 1989. Copyright © by Jerry G. Gaff. By permission of the publishers. All rights reserved.

Middle School Journal for "Problems and Possibilities for an Integrative Curriculum" by James A. Beane. From *Middle School Journal* vol. 25, no. 1, p.18-23, September 1993. Reprinted with permission of *Middle School Journal*. Copyright © 1993 by *Middle School Journal*. All rights reserved.

Instructor magazine for "The Integrated Curriculum" by Heidi Hayes Jacobs. From *Instructor* magazine, vol. 101, no. 2, p. 22-23, September 1991. Copyright © 1991 by Scholastic Inc. Reprinted by permission. All rights reserved.

The Association for Supervision and Curriculum Development for "Integrated Curriculum in Historical Perspective" by Gordon F. Vars. From *Educational Leadership* vol. 49, no. 2, p. 14-15, 1991. Reprinted with permission of the Association for Supervision and Curriculum Development. Copyright © 1991 by ASCD. All rights reserved.

The Oregon School Study Council for "A Comparison of Traditional and Integrative Approaches." From *Integrative Education: A Curriculum for the Twenty-First Century* by Betty Jean Eklund Shoe-

Index

IRI SkyLight
EDUCATIONAL TRAINING AND PUBLISHING

ADDITIONAL RESOURCES TO INCREASE YOUR TEACHING EXPERTISE . . .

The Skylight Catalog

The Skylight Catalog presents a selection of the best publications from nationally recognized authorities on cooperative learning, thinking, assessment, multiple intelligences, and school restructuring. IRI/Skylight offers several other services too!

Training of Trainers

IRI/Skylight provides comprehensive inservice training for experienced educators who are qualified to train other staff members. IRI/Skylight presenters possess years of experience at all levels of education and include authors, field experts, and administrators. IRI/Skylight's training of trainers program is the most powerful and cost-effective way to build the skills of your entire staff.

Training Programs

IRI/Skylight training is available in your district or intermediate agency. Gain practical techniques and strategies for implementing the latest findings from educational research. No matter the topic, IRI/Skylight has an experienced consultant who can design and specially tailor an inservice to meet the needs of your school or organization.

Network

An IRI/Phi Delta Kappa partnership, *The Network of Mindful Schools* is a program of site-based systemic change, built on the core values advocated by Arthur L. Costa. Each member school is committed to restructuring itself to become a "home for the mind." The network is built on three elements: a site leader, a faculty that functions as a team, and an external support system to aid in school transformation.

To receive a free copy of the IRI/Skylight Catalog, find out more about The Network of Mindful Schools, or for more information about trainings offered by IRI/Skylight, contact:

IRI/Skylight Publishing, Inc.

200 E. Wood Street, Suite 274, Palatine, Illinois 60067

800-348-4474
FAX 708-991-6420

There are

one-story intellects,

two-story intellects, and three-story

intellects with skylights. All fact collectors, who have

no aim beyond their facts, are one-story men. Two-story men compare,

reason, generalize, using the labors of the fact collectors as well as their

own. Three-story men idealize, imagine, predict—

their best illumination comes from

above, through the skylight.

—Oliver Wendell

Holmes